# The Winner's Code
## Laws Of A Champion

Thaddeus Parker

2014 Parker Books Trade Paperback Edition

Published in the United States by Parker Books, a division of TDP Holdings LLC.

No parts of the book may be reproduced or used in any fashion without the permission of the author.

Book Cover Design: Myke McKesey, Digital Ink NYC
      info@digitalinknyc.com
Copy Editing: Tanya Tilghman, Can You Picture This
      info@cyptd.com
Photography: Herman Vandenbrandt
      Hermanphoto.net

10 9 8 7 6 5 4 3 2 1

Parker Books
TDP Holdings, LLC.
Wilmington, DE. 19899

Copyright © 2014 Thaddeus Parker

All rights reserved.

ISBN-13: 978-0692217610
ISBN-10: 0692217614

# DEDICATION

I want to dedicate this book to my children; Ryan Lenee, Jeremiah Devon, Levi Devon & Thaddeus Devon Jr. My life's mission is to leave a legacy for you. I'm anxious to see what you all will grow up to be. Without a doubt, I know that you are Champions.

To my mother, Shelia Cannon, I would not be alive today had you not raised me in the admonition of the Lord, instilled morals, values, and the importance of prayer in me. Thank you for giving me your relentless spirit and mantle of ministry.

# ACKNOWLEDGMENTS

This book is a culmination of support from friends, family and mentors from all aspects of my life. For all of them I am eternally thankful.

First and foremost I give all glory and honor to my heavenly father. He is my hero, my undisputed heavyweight champion.

To my great friend, Pastor and bestselling author David Burrus for pushing me to release this overdue book. Thank you!

To my life long friend, Valnique Anderson, who supports all of my crazy ideas 100%. The truth is, I should be reading your literary work. Thank you!

To everyone who sponsored this book with your financial support, I AM FOREVER GRATEFUL.

# CONTENTS

1  Believe You Can      1
2  Let Doubt Go         17
3  Fear Not             35
4  Influence            49
5  Sight Vs. Vision     73
6  Argue The Point      89
7  Define You           115
8  Brand                133
9  Law & Order          161

# PREFACE

This is not a self help book. This is a book of empowerment laws that I believe are necessary ingredients for anyone to win. These laws are based on spiritual and universal principles. Winning is a formula that must be decoded and demystified. As a result, I've divided this book into nine codes packed with history, experiences and principles I know will cause the reader to began winning from the inside out.

# INTRODUCTION

2005

It's a crowd of about 300 people and I'm up in almost thirty minutes. My heart is racing trying to catch up with my thoughts. I planned. I studied. I'm prepared to be transparent and give a wealth of information. I believe I'm ready, yet I'm on edge. I can feel the anticipation in the room. I'm perspiring and it feels like the heat is on hell. When I look up I see with blurred vision a crowd ready to hear me say something life changing. Visibly, this crowd is different from the rest, one being it's the largest. It's not the usual youth cell groups I'm most familiar with. These are a mixture people from all walks of life. I've never done public speaking to this magnitude and time is running from me while the choir sang the last song. Doubt sets in. I began to question my self. Am I ready? Was this a good idea? I should just lean over to the lead pastor and have him choose a more qualified speaker. But why should I do that? After all, I was requested! I'm learned, seminary trained, licensed and ordained. Not to mention, I'm well dressed in a crafted tailored suit with an exceptional solid color tie and paisley hanky accompanied with horn back crocodile shoes…you know, everything I mimicked from the big wigs. I guess I need to come to the reality that I can do this. Okay! I'm ready!

# CODE ONE

# BELIEVE YOU CAN

Much of what we obtain as a people is built on a belief system. Regardless of race, religion, social, or economic background; what we believe has everything to do with our progress in life. Some call it faith and others just plain ole belief. If I were to talk about religion, the topic of discussion would be one's belief in a higher power. If I were to talk about money, the topic of discussion would be one's belief in the financial market. If I were to talk about race, the topic of discussion would be about one's belief in civil rights and social justice. You see, it's impossible to exist without believing in something or someone. In this chapter, my desire is to awaken your consciousness to believe that YOU CAN!

I was fortunate to witness a remarkable event in my lifetime that many fought for, however, didn't live to see come into fruition. The historical election of the first

African American President of the United States inspired the world. On February 10, 2007, just weeks after my daughter was born, I watched national news as then junior senator Barack Obama declared he was running for president. It was on that day where my faith was inspired to aim higher and to go after everything I ever wanted.

I knew that this wasn't just some black guy with a false sense of hope. I knew that this wasn't just another person who had enough time on their hand to run for an office that demanded so much more than the status quo. As I listened to his rather profound and prolific speech and heard the slogan upon which he based his campaign "Yes We Can", it lit a fire in me that still burns today. As a Christian minister, I can recall many scriptural passages that deal with faith, which I will talk about later, however this was monumental.

As I digress, I've had a lot of great moments in my life. Moments of joy, when I prayed with my children and my daughter woke up the next morning and said "Daddy, it looks like God protected us". Moments of sorrow, when I buried patriarchs of my family months apart from each other. Moments of disappointment, moments of love, moments of truth, and moments of rapture. This was a pivotal moment in my life.

I followed the campaign from day one as then, Senator Obama traveled extensively throughout the country with a winning attitude promoting hope and change. I watched carefully as he offed critics and some of the notable politicians who went far beyond the muddy fight of politics and got down right racist. I watched him do so with such integrity. I meditated on the inspirational messages he delivered through speech that seem to seep into the hearts of all kinds of people regardless of race, creed, or background. I gleaned valuable information about the day in which I live. I was proud of what my own race had accomplished after centuries of oppression.

While many wanted to prove to the world how inexperienced he was, I watched him stay true to the mainline issues we faced daily while slipping further into a recession. I watched as he beat one after another both on the republican and democratic side. When he chose Vice President Joe Biden, who happens to be from my home state of Delaware, I watched the vice president exit from his home until he arrived in Chicago to be announced as his running mate. Like many globally, my world changed dramatically and there was no turning back.

It is impossible to talk about the historical election of our first black president without talking about the many black men and woman who paved the way for our president. Marvel Cooke, a journalist, writer, and civil rights activist; Medger Evers, an NAACP official and activist; Malcolm X, a Muslim minister and human rights activist; Martin Luther King, Jr., a Christian minister and human rights activist all were agents of change. These individuals were a handful of many that saw a brighter day and saw no limits. These people believed in something greater than themselves; they believed that we as a people can achieve anything.

Making a difference is what motivates me. Whenever I minister, counsel, or lecture, it's to help others reach their highest potential. It's not enough to have abilities that only benefit you. What is your soul purpose for what you want to do? Your greatest ability to lead is found in your greatest humility to serve. If you're going to be great it would be in your best interest to make sure you are being effective and if you're being effective lives will be changed. It's what I call purpose driven passion. This is not limited to the "who's who" but to the ordinary individual who wants to make a difference. One of my greatest gratifications is to visit homeless shelters to help feed and pray for the less fortunate. There is nothing that compares to that sense of purpose; seeing people who are less fortunate touched, inspired, and changed by servanthood.

Believing produces results. When a person puts their mind to something and begins to believe in themselves, they will experience results. For instance, I began playing piano and the Hammond organ at an early age and for about a year or so I could only play two cords. I managed to play every song with those two cords. If the song was fast, I would play the cords fast and if the song was slow I would simply slow down the tempo. I sucked terribly. I can remember playing one day in frustration and saying to myself "one day I'm going to be good at this". I believed in myself and the gift in me enough that I worked hard, I struggled, but I worked.

There are people that go to school to learn how to read sheet music, which is the best way to excel in the music industry. Then, there are others that can play what they hear by learning the cords through sound, which is my gift. I would get cassette tapes and CD's with a mixture of genres such as gospel, R&B, jazz, country, and learned to play them. My life became consumed in music. I stayed on course until that day came when I made a total living from it.

Who would have ever thought that those two cords would have progressed into a musical career? I did. So one may ask, what am I supposed to do in the in between time of believing I can and destiny? My answer to that person would be, HOLD THE NOTE. I know you must be wondering where in the world am I going with this; allow me to explain. In a band section there is something called tuning. Tuning is a word that is commonly used in music. It simply means to change the pitch of something. When tuning in a band section, a particular instrument holds the note while all other band members match that pitch. In life the most difficult thing at times can be the waiting period. Waiting is a complex word because it means to be inactive or stationary. This definition can be misleading to the degree that a person can mistake being at a standstill with doing nothing. The reality is that standing still and doing nothing are to different things. The attitude we must have in the meantime is to just hold the note while changing the pitch. Working towards your dream while waiting for your big break is holding the note.

Changing the pitch could mean many different things. Perhaps it could mean changing your perception or outlook on a situation. Life and situations aren't always as we perceive them to be and I am a firm believer that if you cannot change a situation then change the way you look at it. The enemy of perception is deception and you can either perceive yourself to be whatever you desire or deceive yourself into believing that it's not possible. Truth has it that all things are possible to those who believe. So now the question I pose to you is how do you see yourself? You have to see yourself there and put yourself there.

Perhaps changing the pitch could mean changing your mind. Often times we as a people can be so closed-minded that we limit ourselves. I can remember when I had my "ah ha moment" and was confronted by someone else in regards to my own "closemindedness." I remember so candidly standing in Borders' Books and Music with a friend in the science section. This particular friend wanted to give me a crash course on Darwin's theory. I've heard of Darwin's theory before but really didn't know what it was about. My initial reaction was to criticize it due to my religious ignorance not realizing that it was okay to learn about something I didn't necessarily agree with. So this individual and I had a show down right there. I proceeded to tell her that she needed to repent before almighty God for suggesting that I even indulge in such conversation. Of course, I was wrong and I was the one who needed to be more open.

Months later, I studied the subject and was enlightened although my theological view did not waiver. Shortly after, I met a group of people in one of my favorite coffee shops and was able to participate in a discussion about it. Just think, had I not changed my mind about gaining knowledge, would I have been able to converse on such a topic or would my ignorance have kept me limited?

Changing the pitch for many could be changing your attitude and again, it determines how far you go. I've been privileged to meet all types of people from various backgrounds and what is interesting are the different personalities. I've rubbed shoulders with wealthy people with the most nasty, inhumane attitudes. I've also met what society considers poor people with such positive, inspirational attitudes and vice versa.

Your attitude determines what you achieve in life, It determines who wants to be around you; your attitude determines who you attract. It determines how well you develop. It determines what type of day you will have. It determines your responses to difficult situations. Your attitude matters! Having the right attitude can give you favor with men and women who can help you reach your goals. Having the wrong attitude will keep you on the loosing team.

You see friends, holding the note is all about change and the use of change in the meantime. One ancient Greek philosopher held that the only thing that's constant in this world is change. The definition of change literally means to alter or to make radically different. There is not one thing about you that you cannot change and a decision can radically change your life forever. No one can define you if your consistent with change. Case and point, people can only define you by what they knew of you for that moment, however, if you're always changing, by the time they try to define you, you would have already transformed into something or someone greater and better. Change should be a consistent part of your lifestyle. Nothing should be overly repetitious. It could be something as simple as challenging yourself on any given day to take a twenty dollar bill to the store just to get change.

The story of Job is one that has transformed me on this matter. This is a story of the most faithful patriarch in the Old Testament who was upstanding and had impeccable moral character. His integrity kept him in right standing with God and did I mention that the guy was loaded with money? I mean literally he was rich. Scriptures record that Satan challenged Job's goodness and received permission from God to test him. When God removed His protection, Satan wiped out his family, health, and his wealth. Here is a guy who lost it all yet understood the importance of the waiting period. Job said "all the days of my appointed time will I wait until my change comes". The benefits of change trumps the reality of a forfeited destiny due to not holding the note. Although there are many crucial elements to this story, I wanted to briefly show you that Job endured the many seasons of his life by holding the note.

Think about it; even seasons change! A year represents a full cycle within a decade and that year according to the calendar is broken up in four consecutive seasons. These seasons are determined by weather and the weather is determined by temperature.

Let's first deal with cycles. In the shortest form, a cycle is repeated phenomenon. Recently when I decided the fate of my success, I sat down and did some extensive assessments and planning. The first area I had to tackle was this issue with repeated phenomenon in my life. I discovered was that there were some good cycles and there were some bad cycles. One of the good cycles is that I've always been able to meet people who had the ability to make things happen. Another good cycle in my life is that I've always been able to bounce back from whatever had the potential to be the end all for me. One of the bad cycles in my life were my choices in women. Another bad cycle I've noticed was the lack of managing my finances with excellence. If you are going to begin the process of believing you can, you must do away with the bad cycles and increase the good ones.

Seasons of life are by far the most important times we cannot afford to take for granted. King Solomon puts it this way…to every thing there is a season, and a time to every purpose under the heaven. More times than not we make decisions in life because we don't recognize what season we are in. People are seasonal, places are seasonal, even the clothes we wear are seasonal. It's crazy to wear a fur coat in the spring or summer time, so then why do we give part time people permanent positions? Why do we confuse a pit stop with our final destination? Just because you dated them doesn't make them your husband or wife and just because a person gives you advice doesn't make them a mentor.

It is a common thing in this day and age to make permanent decisions based on temporary circumstances. Some things only work for the season we are in at that time. If we confuse this important principle, then we will try to reap a harvest in the winter, even though your reaping season should be in the fall.. Have you ever done something for a period of time that seemed to work and then all of a sudden it didn't work anymore? Have you ever worked for a company that seemed to be the dream job and after substantial time there it felt like the job from hell? When a season changes, it will notify you in a thousand ways that particular cycle has run its course. When we don't recognize this vital sign, life becomes fatal. The marvelous thing about seasons is that if you have been in a difficult one lately, just as a season marks the beginning of a thing it also marks the end of the thing.

The common denominator of stormy seasons and seasons of drought is rain. Stormy seasons are the toughest to endure because the variety varies. Take thunderstorms for example. Thunderstorms unlike other storms are most common in the spring and summer, however they can occur in any season of the year. Despite warnings, many people die every single year from the life threatening effects and the most common from this type of storm is lightening from cloud to ground. We also have tornadoes which are violent, dangerous, rotating columns of air in contact with both the surface of the earth and a thunder cloud. The best example in living color for those who haven't actually seen one is shown in the movie entitled *Twister*. Tornadoes are known to literally uproot any and everything in sight and have the power to damage skyscrapers. We also have hurricanes, also known as tropical cyclones, which are a combination of deadly winds, torrential rain, high sea waves, damaging storm surges, and spawning tornadoes.

The season of drought is not like all of the others I have mentioned. The season of drought is a little more complex. According to my research, drought is an extended period of time when a region is deficient of water supply. It drastically impacts the ecosystem and agriculture of that region and causes significant damage. The United Nations estimates that an area of fertile soil the size of Ukraine is lost every year because of drought. This particular season also impacts environmental, agricultural, health, economic and social worlds. Drought impacts lives of every day people. According to my experience, this was actually more difficult than all of the other seasons.

I had to ask myself some real questions like, what do you do when you go from multiple streams of income to none? What do you do when the engagements stop coming in? What do you do when it appears that everything has dried up? I have managed to survive the storms in my life but this storm was the kicker. It was so treacherous that even when I fell back on the many trades I've learned, none really seemed to come through. I'm talking about a season of nothing. Eviction notices were pouring in and reserves were maxed out. This was truly a place I've never been before. While in my drought season it dawned on me that my season changed and I didn't even recognize it.

All of the above are seasons in life and when lived long enough, many have most likely been through just about all of them. Some are thunderous, some are hurricanes, some seem to be huge whirlwinds, some make you eagerly await sunshine while others make you pray for the rain.

Life has a way of teaching us how to weather the storms. There are many who have great tips, classes, and books on how to weather the storms which are all great. I believe the best advice a person can give anyone is to go through the storms, learn the lessons, gain the knowledge, and if you're fortunate enough to come out alive, help someone else.

Out of the four seasons mentioned in a calendar year, one is missing and it's mentioned on God's calendar. This is called due season. Secular society as well as Christianity magnifies the fall season which is reaping season as the most important season, however, let's look at it from another angle. Scripture notes particularly in Galatians 6:9, "and let us not be weary in well doing: for in due season we shall reap, if we faint not." You may have experienced the worst of all seasons but the principle of due season is simple…don't get tired of doing the right thing even in the worst of times. You will overcome and recover. You will win, if you DONT GIVE UP!

Someone once asked, "Thaddeus, are you a thermometer or thermostat?" I paused before responding because I really didn't know which was the right answer. For that matter, I didn't know which one I was. Something about it said "trick question" when actually it was another one of those life changing moments for me. My response was thermometer. The person then told me to look up both meanings so of course I keyed it in Google search. I discovered that a thermometer tells the temperature and a thermostat sets the temperature. This became very interesting and I sat as this individual told me the difference between a person who is a thermometer and a person who is a thermostat.

A person who is a thermometer is controlled by what's going on around them. If the mood is gloomy, they will be gloomy. If the mood is depressing, they will be depressed. If the mood is exciting and full of life then of course they will reflect that energy. This kind of person is always a reflection of what's happening around them with no power to change their environment. Essentially, the environment controls the person.

A person who is a thermostat controls the climate. This person becomes the authority that guides the atmosphere of the room. They assert their power to modify the setting to accommodate the outcome and ultimate success.

There were times that I would walk into a room and was alert enough to tell you who's who and what's what. I could tell who were the movers and shakers, who the protégés were, the wanna be's, and so on. I could tell you what was going on and who was calling the shots. I was a thermometer. After learning, I thought, "if I am to be on top of my "A" game, I need to quickly transform into the person who sets the temperature. I needed too become a thermostat. Now when I walk into an environment, regardless of the venue, I make sure it's working for me. I make my presence known and I modify the energy to fit my existence there.

You can start by going to your favorite store with a vibrant attitude and thought provoking conversation. It will send shockwaves throughout the atmosphere. Watch how quickly people gravitate to you. They will all of a sudden become interested in who you are, what you're about, and what you have to say. That's your opportunity to push your brand and engage your listener. When you are a thermometer, you set limits for yourself to the possibilities of success. The greatness of this principle is that no matter where you are in life, no matter what your position is, you can make the change. You have to decide which one you will be and if you are passionate about your dreams and goals, you will make the right choice.

I've already given you five important steps to believing you can. Let's recap.

1. Hold the note.
2. Be consistent with change
3. Know what season your in.
4. Identify and weather your storms.
5. Set the temperature.

## CODE TWO

## LET DOUBT GO

*Cast not away therefore your confidence, which hath great recompense of reward.*

- Hebrews 10:35

Let nothing and no one cause you to throw away your confidence. There are great benefits of having self assurance that will pay off in the long run. No one can believe in you, your dreams, or your ideas like you can. You have to be your biggest cheerleader, rooting for yourself, knowing who you are, and what you are capable of. There is greatness in you and you must be sure. You must be tenacious. You must be driven. You must be optimistic…have a winning attitude and you will win!

One might ask, how can I find the champion in me? How can I win in life? My rebuttal is always a confrontation of the lie either someone told them or they told their self. Who told you that you weren't great? Who told you that you are a failure? Who told you that it was impossible? Was it someone else or was it you? There is nothing like you doubting you as opposed to someone else, such as a teacher, friend, enemy, or even a family member. The effect is greater when it's you opposing you. So let's confront the enemy of confidence, let's confront self-doubt.

Self-doubt has been something I've struggled with, from feeling I was not like all the other kids to feeling rejected. I bought into the inner critic that aided to my already existing fear. Even with all of my knowledge of self esteem, I felt inadequate. In reality, it is a normal thing in our humanity to feel as such. For some it's worse than others and could be based on a number of things.

One of the reasons, simply put, is that we are not exempt from humanity. We are fleshly beings who have emotions predicated on our five senses. One of the realities of being a human being is that we will thrive off of how we feel at the moment. Circumstances of life will sometimes cause us to retract and retreat on the very things we know we were born to do. It's all due to the opposition called doubt.

Doubt is a disease that will slowly eat away at your destiny like cancer does the body. It will target the mind because that's where creativity lives. Doubt will target your heart because that's where your goodwill and passion lives. It will get down in your soul and slowly chip away because that's where you are connected with God. If you permit it, doubt will get into every fiber of your being until you are nothing more than a walking corps.

There are many effects of self-doubt. A few of these could be the feeling of isolation, intimidation, and fear, all of which I had to confront in order to conquer. Doubt caused me to be anti-social and I felt alone in the world. I thought my difference was some sort of disease. It never dawned on me that there are no two identical people in the universe. My mother has an identical twin sister and for many years my friends could not tell them apart yet it was clear to all who knew us that they were in many fashions total opposite. They look alike, in most ways act alike, often do everything together but they are not the same person.

Greater than that I had to get to the root of my loneliness and mine stemmed from my early childhood. For instance, when all the other kids would go out to play, I would stay in the house. I can recall many times when my parents would make me go out to play with all of the other kids. As I grew older it progressed.

As I researched isolation what stood out to me most is the term "solitary confinement". You will see this term used in the state and federal prison system. Solitary confinement is a special form of imprisonment in which a prisoner is denied or given limited contact with any other person. A light bulb went off in my head and it dawned on me that we can be confined within in our own skin until we make the decision to be comfortable with who we are and our uniqueness.

It's ok to be different. Many get being different mistaken for being abnormal. Today's culture has a way of convincing us that having our own uniqueness is irregular. We must challenge what suggests that we have to be like everyone else or do what everyone else is doing. Embrace the fact that you are different rather than fit in a system of normalcy. The moment I embraced this philosophy I became a better me. No longer do I doubt myself and I have the confidence to do whatever my mind can conceive.

There are many treasures inside of you that will never be discovered if you don't believe in yourself. You can be whatever you desire to be in this world but it's going to take confidence. Confidence gives you the power needed to do something without the fear of failing or being good enough. The God of creation is the giver of dreams so you have to be confident in what He placed in you. When you are self-confident, you acknowledge that you have the capacity to complete a task and not run away from it because of fear.

When you become self-confident, you don't need anyone to validate who you are. You validate yourself. You do not seek the approval of others. You are comfortable in your shell and you use inner strength to make it happen. Evidence of self confidence is a person with guts. These individuals pursue and take advantage of all opportunities even at their own risk. Being successful takes an enormous amount of plain ole guts.

One of the ways I defeated self-doubt was to identify my strengths and weaknesses; once I did I maximized my ability to succeed by capitalizing from the two. Your greatest strength is knowing your weakness. When you identify what your weakness is, it will become your strength. It's simple; if you know that you can cook but you're not good in finance, owning a restaurant without having an accountant wouldn't be wise. Whatever your not strong in, hire someone else to do.

Confidence doesn't make you a perfect being. There are many imperfection in our humanity so don't expect everything to be perfect. Instead, use self confidence as a torch to keep you going when others see you stopping.

The worse thing anyone can do is doubt ones own self. While attending a Farrah Gray session in Philadelphia, I heard him say "it's amazing what a person can do when they don't know what they can't do". I thought wow, so true. My daughter and I have a healthy relationship and because she has an interesting imagination, it makes for constant daddy and daughter talks. I'm teaching her about the devil called "CAN'T". It is a word that is forbidden in my house and our vocabulary. Her imagination is adventurous and full of life. Whenever we have our moments to share I tell her how important it is to never use that word "can't". As my sons vastly approach their time to share with daddy, they too will learn of this devil. You see "can't" is a word that limits your way of thinking which ultimately limits your ability. Using that word will never have a positive impact that's conducive to succeeding. It will always remind you of the impossible when truth has it, nothing is impossible.

I was about eight years old when I had my first encounter with rejection. It was a long saga that would send my life in a world spin. I remember this day as if it were yesterday, one that I will never forget. I was hanging with my siblings and some of my cousins and like every family who has an aunt or uncle who's an alcoholic, I had one of those crazy cousins. I'm talking crazy, silly, loud, and disruptive. Fun to be with, but a person who at times was notorious for being a nuisance.

While hanging around as we did often because we are a very close family, my cousin implied that she had some family secrets. Our attention was summonsed as she told a story she could have only over heard the grown folk talking about. Among the secrets were; the only father I knew was not my real father. While those who were present were shocked, I was crushed, hurt, and confused. My proceeding thought was that this cannot be true. The man who taught me how to tie a tie, the man who taught me how to fish, the only dad I knew was not in fact my biological father?

Determined to know the truth, I waited for the right time to ask my mom the big question. Was daddy really my dad? I remember vividly; we were riding down Fourth Street passing Delaware Technical Community College on our way home. The car was a white Ford Tempo and while sitting in the back nervously I asked, "is my dad my real dad?"

After my mother demanded I tell where I got such information, she then replied with the big answer. No. Now I'm really curious as to what in the hell has been going on. So I have another question…"what's my real dad's name?" My mother replied. "his name is Timothy." I could sense that this was not something my mother was ready to talk about and I didn't say anymore. I figured that when she is ready to come clean, she would.

A few years went by and one day I skipped school in the seventh grade and decided I would go hang out at my Godmother's (who was actually an older cousin) house. My Godmother was just cool and her house was the hangout spot. She was much older than me and in my quest to find out about my real dad I asked my Godmother if she knew of him. She was forthcoming in that she remembers him and both he and my mom dating. So I thought cool. Then I probed for more information only to find out that I look and act like him. What's more alarming was that I found out that his name was not Timothy. My biological father's name is Thaddeus and I was named after him.

At this point I'm not only confused, now I'm angry. Why would my mother tell me his name was Timothy? Which one is it? So when I got home, I asked her again. What is my dad's name? She then replied that his name is Thaddeus. The most devastating thing of it all was that she said she did not remember telling me his name is Timothy. She acknowledged that his nickname is Tim, but that in fact what my Godmother said was true. His name is Thaddeus Riggins and my name is Thaddeus Parker. I was given my mother's maiden name because she lived by an old school rule that said if you're not married then the child doesn't get the father's last name. I've personally never heard or agree with something so ridiculous.

She proceeded to tell me her version of what happened. I was born July 1, 1986 and shortly before that my mother and father split. In the short time span of about six months after I was born, my mom somehow managed to move on and marry the man who I thought was my dad. From that point the feeling of rejection would overpower me in ways that are unexplainable. I would asked myself over and over why didn't Thaddeus want me? Why didn't he send for me? Was I not good enough to be his son?

It would not be until years later after already pastoring my first church and being married to my first wife, all at age nineteen, that I finally get to meet Thaddeus Riggins. I woke up one day and decided that I could not possibly go on with my life until I knew where I came from. I could not embrace wholeheartedly my destiny until I knew my history. I called my mom on the phone and told her that this is the day where it all ends. I told her to get dressed because I was on my way.

I arrive that morning at my parent's house to discover that she and my dad, as I knew him, are ready but not sure as to where we are going. I explain to them that today we were going to find my dad but before we left I needed to know everything mom remembered. What was the last thing you remember about him? What is the last known address that you have for him? What's my grandparents' name? Do I have any aunts and uncles? My mother responded that the only thing she can remember without a doubt is that my grandmother lived a few blocks away from the Trenton, New Jersey train station. She recalled times when the two of them were dating where they frequently boarded the train to visit his mother and that they would get off the train and walk two blocks down.

That was all I needed to hear, so I devised the plan. We get in my car and proceed to drive from Wilmington, Delaware to Trenton, New Jersey. When we arrive at the train station, we ask one of the employees for a map, hoping that it would help mom remember a little better being as though everything was very different since she had last been there in the mid 1980's. That was a twenty year gap. We were able to gauge what direction to go and when we arrived to the suspected place, there was only one residential block left partially filled with town homes.

Mom couldn't remember much else so I decided that I would start knocking on doors. The very first door I knock on, an elderly woman, who would later share that she was eighty seven years old, answered. I know that three complete strangers at her door would catch her by surprise so I immediately tell her that I'm in search of my family who we believed live on this block. She asked for their name and so I gave her my father's name. When she heard the name it all came together.

Her daughter and my father's sister happened to be close friends. My grandmother no longer lived at that address and the house she once owned on the block was torn down. Nothing existed on that part of the block but a parking lot. The elderly woman stated that my grandmother was in a nursing home and that my aunt and her daughter were doing grocery shopping together the week prior. She took down my information to forward. We graciously thanked her and drove back to Delaware. About an hour after I got home my phone started to ring with all of my family members whom I've never met.

It would be hours later after speaking with a number of family members including siblings I never knew before I get "the call". This call was the most anticipated call…the call where the two Thaddeus's would finally meet again. After all, there is a lot of catching up to do. The phone rang and I answered. On the other end was a strong southern voice that said "son, it's your dad." At that moment, the anger and bitterness I had towards him had withered away and we began to share. It all started with a voice and four words, and after talking for hours, we decided to meet.

Weeks later would be the first time I would come face to face with the man whom others say I reflect and the father who abandoned me. He was scheduled for a road trip from where he lives in Charleston, South Carolina to New Jersey and we agreed to meet at that time. We talked often leading up to that day. On a fall night in October, I met my dad. I finally got the chance to lay eyes on him. I saw me in him and him in me. We had so much in common. It was rather odd at times because we often did and said the same thing. He thought he was "GQ" and I knew that I was. He thought that he was the man and so did I. More importantly, I got the chance to ask all of the questions and he gave me all of the answers to my questions. We laughed and we cried. That was the night that I got closure.

Rejection is a hard pill to swallow. I mean who really wants to deal with the emotion that comes with it? Whether it is in relationships, friendships, partnerships…the feeling of not being wanted will cause you to doubt yourself. Rejection has a brutal sting but it is full of lessons. It's all in what you do with the feeling that determines how you overcome. You can overcome rejection by understanding that there is a divine purpose. It could be that God wanted you to evolve without the other person's interference.

I now see rejection as one door shutting and another door opening. When I was rejected in the area of relationship, I took what love I had left, healed, and moved on. When I was rejected in business, I took the lessons learned and used that wisdom to expand. There is always room to grow.

Having worked in the manufacturing industry and on production lines, occasionally while making a product we would come across rejects. Rejects were products considered to be defective and deemed not useful which prevented it from becoming a finished product. In the production line of creation when God was manufacturing us, He made us just right to become the finished product. You are not a reject and just because you've experienced rejection in life does not constitute you to be so.

## THE PROCESS OF BECOMING

When you break up with doubt you start the "process of becoming". You will not wake up and be everything you desire. You will not be the best man, woman, student or perhaps CEO overnight. The process of becoming suggests that you are being developed on a consistent basis thus improving you from the inside out. This will mean that you are being adjusted for the best possible results. The dawning moment when you can say that "I'm not there" is the moment you acknowledge that you are still progressing.

Everything takes time. Before a child is born he or she must stay in the womb for a period of nine months to be developed. Before any one becomes a doctor they must go through twelve years of grade school and another eight years of college. To build relationships and partnerships properly will demand the essence of time. You must put in the necessary time to become what you desire.

Consider Oprah Winfrey for a moment. She is highly respected as one of the world's top media tycoons. Her story as an African American woman is one that is without a doubt remarkable. She grew up in a time of racial and gender discrimination in the heart of the south. She was raised by her father, became promiscuous, became pregnant in her teens, had a period of drug use, and had a history of being in dysfunctional relationships with men.

After college, she pursued a career in broadcasting and was told that she would never excel because her eyes were too far apart. While working at a television station in Baltimore, Maryland, she accepted a position in

Chicago that catapulted her career to worldwide stardom and success. Before we ever knew her as Oprah, before she ever out rated everyone in daytime talk shows like veteran Phil Donahue, before she ever had her own magazine or satellite radio show, all that she experienced before arriving in Chicago was her process of becoming. It would be good to note that even after holding the number one spot for twenty-five years and transitioning to the launch of her own television network, that even that took two years to receive favorable ratings. Today she is a billionaire.

There is a term widely used called character maintenance. You will discover a plethora of descriptions of this term, however I want to hone in on this particular one…the fine tuning of one's character. Individuals who are in the process of becoming must understand that there are a series of transformations before being "you" at your best.

Character maintenance says you will consistently do self checks without beating yourself up. One example is that if you make a mistake, rather than coming down on yourself, learn the lessons of the mistake and move on. This will build you up and improve your character. Your character will tell those around you how disciplined you really are.

Character maintenance is based on the concept that individuals can be their best critic. When you are your best critic, the criticism of others is secondary. There are two types of criticisms; the first being constructive, and the second being destructive. Constructive criticism targets the issue. Destructive criticism targets the person. When critiquing yourself constructively, it will never have a negative effect but rather improve you in unimaginable ways. Criticism is a technique.

## KEEP A SKEPTIC ON YOUR TEAM

Jesus assembles His cabinet of twelve. He has the rather difficult task to hand pick His team. This team must be a group that can handle the weight of spiritual diplomacy. He chooses twelve because throughout time, history has proved it to be the number of systematic order.

In mathematics, twelve is a composite number; the smallest number with exactly six divisors, its divisors being 1, 2, 3, 4, 6 and 12. There are twelve months in a year. There are twelve numerical numbers on a clock that establish order to a complete cycle of a day. The human body has twelve cranial nerves. The western zodiac has twelve signs. There are twelve tribes of Israel. There are twelve gates in heaven. The woman with the issue of blood found in Luke's gospel (Luke 8:43) lived with that issue for twelve years.

As Jesus prepares for ministry, He becomes a master strategist as He chooses the twelve that will carry out His agenda. The twelve He selects have their own uniqueness and all of them have strengths, skills, and weaknesses. Some even have occupations... Matthew, a tax collector; Peter, a fisherman (the most controversial one); Andrew, the brother of Peter; and John, the great revelator, to name a few.

What has a great deal of importance is that out of the twelve, Jesus chose Thomas. The big question is why does Jesus pick Thomas? It's just as mysterious as to why He chose Judas knowing that he would betray Him or even Peter whom He knew would ultimately deny Him. But a guy of this magnitude has to know what He's doing. Thomas is not your ordinary guy. He's gifted enough to be apart of the cabinet but no matter how much you show him, he's still a skeptic.

Skepticism is the method of suspended judgment, systematic doubt, or criticism characteristic of skeptics. There are two types of skepticism. The first being ordinary skepticism and the second being philosophical skepticism. Ordinary skepticism would suggest that because there is a lack of appearance, it's easy to doubt what one cannot see. For instance, if I told you that I was a millionaire yet I do not have the bells and whistles of a millionaire, it would be hard to believe. It is that "see it to believe it" syndrome.

In contrast, you have philosophical skepticism which seeks to rationalize based on given information. For example, if I said I was a millionaire, philosophical skepticism would inquire who, what, and how. The scenario would be; my name is Tim Johnson and I'm the CEO of Johnson & Co. Through business achievements, I've amassed millions. Without the "reason" or the "how" I have a million dollars would cause for reasonable doubt.

In today's culture, people will doubt you based on these two examples; either by appearance or information. I cannot say the same about why Thomas infamously known as "doubting Thomas" was a skeptic. Here is a guy who was with Jesus during many of the miracles He performed. He saw Jesus do impossible things like heal blind eyes, feed the multitudes, and perhaps walk on water. However when it came to him believing that Jesus appeared in the upper room after death and resurrection, he was a skeptic.

Still the question lingers, why did Jesus choose Thomas knowing his proclivity to doubt. As many would debate as to why, I cannot say that I have the answer. It is my hypothesis that if one set out to do impossible things, then a necessary individual to keep close is one who is skeptical for self motivation. After all, what you do should look effortless to those who do not see how you are going to get it done.

# CODE THREE

# FEAR NOT

*"Our Deepest fear is not that we are inadequate. Our deepest fear is that we are powerful beyond measure".*

*- Marianne Williamson*

September 11, 2001...the world as we have known it would change forever. It was certainly a day that I will never forget. I believe anyone who was alive remembers the details of their life that day. I was a freshman at Brandywine High School and the school year had just started. It was a big difference from middle school in which I came from just a few months prior and I now had to be acclimated to a new building, new faculty, and a much larger student body. Among the usual courses I took up music theory, electronics and carpentry. Although I didn't stick with electronics, music theory and carpentry held my interest.

On this particular morning, I go through the normal routine of waking up early, getting dressed, getting on the school bus and making my way to school. I went to breakfast and ate fruit with oatmeal then off to homeroom. The bell rang and now it's time for my first class. This class happens to be carpentry. I walk in sit down and received instructions to choose a partner. Ironically, I was cool with a classmate who also was named Thaddeus. Thaddeus Black was his name and we decided to hook up, as we were to start the project of the day. My school was very modern and on the cutting edge and so it wasn't out of the ordinary to have televisions mounted in the classrooms and this particular teacher always kept it on the news.

About twenty minutes or so into the class, the teacher tells us to quiet down as his attention shifts dramatically to what was happening on TV. We could see that something shifted in his demeanor. The look on his face said something was seriously wrong. At this point our faces are glued to the television, not sure of what exactly is going on, but we knew that whatever was happening was major. At first glance, there is a very tall building with smoke emerging vigorously from it and my thought was, "what in the world is going on?" Then we see with our own eyes the second plane hit the twin towers (The World Trade Center).

Immediately, the sense of fear would over shadow the country we all were in a state of shock. We didn't know what was happening but what was clear, was that the planes had hit the buildings. As we continued to watch, we saw the once on looking crowds suddenly running away from the smoking buildings as they began tumbling down. With limited details, the reign of terror and fear had gripped us all. It wouldn't be long after, that the principal would come on the loud speaker to announce our early dismissal.

Once home I was greeted on the porch by my parents who wanted to ensure that my older brother who was a senior at the high school we attended and I were ok. Collectively, we would all gather in the living room to continue to watch the news as details unfolded. We learned at this point that the Pentagon was also hit by a plane and also that another plane had crashed in Pennsylvania. That plane was deemed to be terrorist controlled. The newscasters confirmed earlier speculations that this had in fact been a terrorist attack on our nation. No one thought that this could ever happen in the most powerful country in the world.

After a while my mother turned off the TV and as it was common practice in our house, we joined hands and prayed. My mother has always been one who could pray in such a way, you'd feel the hair stand up on your body. With our heads bowed, we listen as she would thank God for grace, mercy, and even though we didn't know what quite was going on in the world, he was still God. She went on to tell God that we trust Him on this day of uncertainty. She prayed for those who lost loved ones, that God would be with them. She prayed for peace in our nation, and guidance for our nation's leader. It was a riveting experience and at the end, we all concluded with "amen." That day not only did my immediate family pray, the world came together in unity to host prayer vigils and services literally around the world. But that fear still loomed over us.

Days later in the midst of the greatest tragedy America had seen since the attack on Pearl Harbor, we were faced with another scare. This was the anthrax situation. While it was clear that terrorist attacked us using airplanes, it was unclear whether or not it was terrorists who were sending a deadly powder-like substance in the mail. This particular attack wasn't due to airplanes but it seemed to have been traveling by air as well. Anthrax would make its debut in New Jersey and even travel to two United States Democratic Senators' offices. At a time when the world prayed that things would somehow get better, it appeared to get worse.

I recall the fear being intense. No one, not even the elected officials or the president himself seemed to have the power to make things better. Presidential adviser Carl Rove suggested to President Bush that speaking to first responders was the right thing to do. It was at that moment when we saw our commander-in-chief get right in the middle of chaos and speak from the heart with such grace and strength. This wasn't like the speech he delivered from the Oval Office just three days prior. Although I was never a fan of former president George W. Bush, I commend him for standing on the rubble of ground zero that day and delivering the famous bullhorn speech. Yet and still, fear and anguish had a choke hold on the world.

## *"Only Thing We Have to Fear Is Fear Itself"*

### *-Franklin D. Roosevelt*

There is another catastrophe that our country faced known as the Great Depression. 1929 saw the greatest recession the world has ever known. Stock markets began to decline at an unstoppable rate and eventually crashed in October of that year. It was indeed the longest and deepest recession in western industrialism. Wall Street went into panic and it was estimated that millions of investors were completely wiped out. Over the course of a decade consumer spending and investments had nearly vanished causing major declines in industrialism, forcing companies to lay off employees. When the Great Depression reached its peak, nearly fifteen million people were unemployed. Not to mention that half of the country's banks and financial institutions had gone under.

I read of stories of how people were literally killing themselves in gruesome ways. There were accounts of people jumping off building, bridges and even out of the windows of high rises. These people didn't fear losing it all, they lost it all. There were no government programs and the only relief at that time were charities such as the Salvation Army, which provided food and shelter.

Herbert Hoover, a republican, was president at the start of the depression. He believed that if you were in trouble you should help yourself and not expect others to help you. This was what he called "rugged individualism". He did not do a great deal to help those who were unemployed. It was President Hoover's philosophy that "it is not the function of the government to relieve individuals of their responsibilities to their neighbors, or to relieve private institutions of their responsibilities to the public."

President Hoover also did not believe that the depression would last. "Prosperity is just around the corner" is what he said to businessmen in 1932 just as the horror was getting worse. It was on this basis that Franklin Roosevelt launched a campaign against Hoover and won by a land slide victory.

After his election President Roosevelt, a democrat, would confront enemy number one to the recovery of the economy, which was fear. Fear had saturated people from all backgrounds and for a while everyone shared the same financial status. President Roosevelt looked at his country with eyes of optimism and saw a restored economy, a restored world, and more importantly a restored people. Although it did not happen overnight, he knew that if the people would start existing outside the perimeters of fear than they could recover. So he began his first state of the union address where the famous quote was derived. His philosophy was to only fear fear itself.

The greatest thing that stops people from chasing their dream is fear. Fear is a scare tactic that Satan use to keep people with purpose complacent and never wondering what it's like on the other side. There is another side of failure and that's success. There is another side of poverty and it is prosperity. There is another side of grief and it is happiness. But as long as fear has its grasp, one will never entertain the thought of getting to the other side. Fear itself, when given permission, sabotages God's original plan for ones life. Some say embrace fear, others say fear is your friend, President Roosevelt said to fear fear. I say FEAR NOT!

People who have innovative ideas usually never attempt to make things happen because they fear failure and or success. The two are related conditions. What if my idea isn't good enough? What if it doesn't work? Or on the flip side, what if it does work? My research led me to the word *atychiphobia*. Atychiphobia is the unusual, unwarranted, and ongoing fear of failure and/or success. As with many phobias, atychiphobia often leads to a constricted lifestyle, and is particularly devastating for it affects a person's willingness to attempt certain activities.

A person afflicted with atychiphobia considers the possibility of failure so intensely that they choose not to take a chance. Often this person will subconsciously undermine their own ability so that they no longer have to continue to try. Because effort is proportionate to the achievement of personal goals and fulfillment, this unwillingness to try that arises from the perceived inequality between the possibilities of success and failure holds the atychiphobic back from the realization of potential.

Fear is not your friend. Fear will cause you to live to be eighty years old, have children, have grand children, work a job, retire from that job and even collect social security only to discover that you have never in your life gone after anything. Fear will allow you to live aimlessly. Fear will sign your permission slip to live life without purpose and before you know it, life will have passed you by.

Fear doesn't exist in the mind of winner's. Neither is it a part of our language. In fact, fear will systematically prevent you from winning. The last thing you want to do is allow fear to even be an option. To control fear means to understand fear and how it works. Fear works like a consuming fire torching everything you want to accomplish for you and those you love. When fear is eradicated, opportunities are endless. Here are five critical things that fear impacts.

1. **Intuition.** I call it "your knower". Intuition is the ability to understand something immediately, without the need for conscious reasoning. Your gut could be telling you to do what your most passionate about. The idea for someone or even yourself to try and talk you out of it is senseless because down in your knower, this is what you are supposed to do. Sound intuition will convey data objectively. Sound intuition will give you clear premonition. Fear then will come along in disguise of reason and give every so-called good reason why you shouldn't do it. Fear will make you believe that your intuition is nothing more than pure allusion. Let what you know in your knower guide you and sooner than later you will find out that it was God the whole time.

2. **Emotions.** Your emotions are a subjective expression of your current state of mind. What you are thinking will ultimately exude outwardly what is going on inwardly. Fear driven emotions are simply anxiety that paralyzes the mobility of your life. A few negative impacts of fear-laced emotions are depression, panic attacks, and emotional breakdowns.

3. **Perception.** How you view life, the world, and culture are extremely important. Fear will not allow you to see the things that are most crucial to winning such as opportunity, options, and creativity. Fear will put a haze like effect on your view and all that you see will be blurred.

4. **Connections.** Personal relationships run the world and making connections is a must. Regardless if you're in ministry, business, or politics, there is no way of getting around it if you're intentional about winning. Fear will

impact who you connect with. There are people with innate abilities that you can benefit from but if you have a social fear, those connections won't be made.

5. **Progress.** Progress is the ability to move towards a place. Fear ultimately in the end stops your progress. If fear can put you in an emotionally distraught state, alter your perception and cause you not to make the necessary connections, then there will be no progress. You will never get to that desired place.

## FEED YOUR FAITH. STARVE YOUR FEAR.

*For God hath not given us the spirit of fear; but of power, and of love, and of a sound mind. - 2Timothy 1:7*

Faith is one of my favorite subjects to talk about and I could spend days talking about the nuances of faith. I have for the last decade been an advocate for people seeing themselves as champions and having a winning attitude. This was founded on the principle that in order to live like a "champ" or otherwise known as one that has a consistent track record of winning; it is done by faith and faith alone.

Faith is a much talked about subject and its meaning varies according to the one who's talking. You will hear many diverse definitions and analogies; for example, faith is one's belief in self or faith is one's belief in a higher power. But from a biblical perspective, it's clear on what faith is and what faith is not.

*Now faith is the substance of things hoped for and the evidence of things not seen.  -Hebrews 11:1*

I sometimes converse with my clergy counterparts with regards to this subject. One of my challenges with the so called "word of faith" movement is that without notice the philosophy put emphasis on having faith in faith rather than having faith in God. You would hear ministers say catchy clichés like " stay faithful to faith". However, the scriptures say have faith in God.

Abraham is a familiar figure and one who knows something about this thing called faith. In Genesis 12, Abraham receives divine direction to get out of his country and away from his family to go to a place that had not been revealed. The first challenge is that he has to leave the only place he's ever known. That wouldn't be a deal breaker for some as starting over in a new place would be a breath of fresh air. The second challenge is to leave everyone he loves behind. Now this can be problematic for some because we tend to believe that the people in our lives today were meant to be there tomorrow. But here's where the problem is…how do I start a journey with no intended destination?

It's like getting up in the morning, getting showered and dressed. You get the kids ready and everyone eats breakfast. You then get in the car and start it up with no where to go. Essentially, that was Abraham's faith challenge. He had greatness on him. He's loaded with vision. He has specific instructions but he doesn't know where he's going. What detail Abraham does know is that although he does not know where destiny is, he's sure that God will show him.

Now imagine, if you just take the first step at what you were created to do knowing God is leading you. To be fearful would make sense if you were leading yourself but if God is ordering your steps, why aren't you moving forward? What's holding you back? You are too gifted to be standing around waiting for something to happen. You have to be fearless. You must go get it at the cost of not knowing where you will end up.

With every faith challenge is an attached promise. God brokers the deal with Abraham and tell him to hit the road and when he does; one, He will create a great nation out of him. Secondly, He will bless him. Third, He would make him famous. Fourth, He will give him so much that he's able to give to others. Then the deal gets really good. Next, He tells Abraham He will bless those who would dare bless him but whoever curses him, will be cursed. Lastly, everyone will benefit from this deal.

Launch the company. Go back to school. Record the album. Whatever your life's purpose is, get in the car and hit the road. You are the seed of Abraham and every promise he received from God is now yours. Forget about what you don't have and focus on what you do have. As long as you have four wheels on the car, drive!

Don't look back because what's in front of you is far greater than what is behind you. So what you're unsure where you will end up; keep driving and don't stop.

After signing the deal with God and leaving, he would eventually pass through a place called Shechem. Shechem historically was the place where foolish people dwelled. Sometimes when you make a faith move you will have to encounters foolish people and foolish situations, but it's not for you to stay and be frustrated. Abram kept it moving. That's exactly what you have to do no matter what opposes you.

To keep moving even in the face of adversity, you have to feed your faith. God's word must become your diet. Your appetite will change and the things that you used to consume will no longer suffice. Faith comes by hearing on a continuous basis the word of God. If you would dare feed your faith, then fear will have no other choice but to die.

Fear is the opposite of faith. Faith produces and fear kills. Faith says pursue destiny as if you were a blind man. A blind man feels his way onward with the hope of getting to where he needs to be. He doesn't have time to fear. He doesn't have time to wonder because he's to busy wandering his way to his destination. Having faith in God knowing He's got you becomes your most lucrative insurance policy.

You must be wondering by now, when will I know

that I arrived to the place where I need to be? When I was a little boy my mother use to send my siblings and I to the corner store. If that store didn't have what she wanted, we would have to go to various local stores some blocks away. The times when we were unsure of how to get there, she would give us directions with landmarks. She would always conclude the directions with "you will know it when you get there". How do you know that you arrived? That I do not know but, you will know it when you get there.

# CODE FOUR

# INFLUENCE

It was in 2009 on a Saturday night that I initially had plans to go out when all of a sudden my plans changed. So I thought what do I do now? Ready and now having nothing in the world to do, I grab the remote control. While flipping through the channels, I first stop to watch a movie realizing a few minutes in that it was uninteresting partly due to the fact that I'm an action movie kind of guy and this certainly wasn't an action film. As I continue browsing through channels I land on CNN. This night they were doing a documentary on Jim Jones entitled *Escape From Jonestown*.

The documentary told a haunting tale about a religious leader and community activist who founded the Peoples' Temple. Jim Jones being born in Indiana started the Temple there in the 1950s. He later moved the Temple to California in the mid-1960s, and gained notoriety with the move of the Temple's headquarters to San Francisco in the early 1970s.

The show went on to detail that Jones was a voracious reader as a child and studied the likes of Joseph Stalin, Karl Marx, Mahatma Gandhi and Adolf Hitler to understand each of their strengths and weaknesses. Jones also developed an intense interest in religion, primarily because he found making friends difficult. Childhood acquaintances later recalled Jones as being strange and having a strong liking with religion and being overly curious with death. I later read that those who knew him up close alleged that he frequently held funerals for small animals on his parents' property.

All of this became very interesting to me as I've heard about him in times past but never really paid it much attention. After all, this did take place eight years before I was born. My attention is now engrossed in the documentary as it went on to describe the mind of this guy. On one extreme, he is troubled as a child with a rather sick mind and on the other extreme he is a educated married man who had a keen love for people.

After hearing a speech about the plight of African American people by Eleanor Roosevelt, Jones was intrigued. It was then that his love for religion would soon become an opportunity to pastor in the Methodist church. Later claims suggest that he would leave the denomination to start his own movement because at that time, the Methodist sect would not let him integrate blacks into his congregation. Jones, who also studied other denominations and various styles of preaching, concluded that a mixture of charisma, faith healing, civil and human rights activism was extremely persuasive. As a result, it wouldn't take long for his church and influence to grow at a fast rate.

Jones' true desire came to light as his narcissism would shift his followers from being the community congregation that fought for social justice, to being loyal and obedient to Jones. He eventually came under government and media scrutiny for rumors of sexual and physical abuse. In 1977, Jones moved the Peoples' Temple to Guyana, where his team built their own utopia: Jonestown. Jones convinced members of his church to sell their homes, sign over their paychecks and life savings to the movement.

Nearly 1,000 people followed Jones to Jonestown, supposedly a well-planned community with a clinic, school and communal kitchen. Over time, Jones' behavior became alarming. It was rumored he was abusing drugs, and he would give speeches over a loud speaker that were said to be increasingly frantic.

Back at home in the United States, family members became increasingly concerned that their loved ones were being held against their will and went to their local officials. It was at this time that then Representative Leo Ryan of California traveled to investigate the allegations of Jonestown. When it became clear that something was wrong he decided to take his findings back to the United States.

The facts were that Jonestown was no utopia, neither was it a place where peace and tranquility existed, but rather a place of extreme control and terror ran by a dictator. Although Jones seemed to be calm in the presence of Representative Ryan, he knew that his days were coming to an end if in fact those fact-findings reached Washington. Enraged, paranoid, and under heavy cocaine intoxication, Jones ordered a hit on Representative Ryan and those who accompanied him at the airstrip where their plane was stationed.

Meanwhile, back at Jonestown, Jim Jones called an emergency meeting. He convinced his followers to drink the infamous cyanide laced kool-aid starting with the babies and children first and then adults. That day over nine hundred people died and the worst part of it all was that Jim Jones himself did not die of the same method that he had convinced others. Like the coward he was, he shot himself and died of a self-inflicted wound.

I guess you can imagine that after watching the documentary that night my understanding of influence had a whole new meaning. About a year or so later, I watched on the Oprah show as a man talked about his father and gave further insight into the mind of such a man. Oprah was actually interviewing Jim Jones, Jr. He would tell of how he was an African American child adopted by Caucasian parents. Jones Jr. grew up not thinking anything of it because in his family, they did not see color.

Jim Jones Jr. shared that he was seventeen when he went with his father to Guyana. He recalled that he was in Georgetown, Guyana at age eighteen playing in a basketball tournament which is a hundred and fifty miles away from where the mass suicide took place. When his father told him what was about to happen via radio, he and his teammates went to the U.S. Embassy to try to prevent the massacre thinking that they could do something to stop it. He then reveals that among the nine hundred and some odd people who died were his parents, brother, sister, wife and unborn child.

As bazaar as this story sounds, I had to ask myself how can one man convince that many people that he could lead them into a false world of non-existent reality. My conclusion is that he could have only accomplished such by using the power of influence. If Jim Jones could use influence in such an inhumane way, what more could those of us who are dreamers do?

Influence is one of the most powerful forces on earth. Influence effects culture and it occurs when one's emotions, opinions, or behaviors are affected by others. No one regardless of what you do for a living can say that you were not influenced by someone. Michael Jackson, the king of pop was influenced by James Brown, the godfather of soul. Nat King Cole influenced Marvin Gaye. Johnny Carson influenced David Letterman. The resolve to win is based on the power of influence. Who you listen to you will soon become. What you watch controls the eyes of the imagination. Who you follow matters, even on social media.

Most people will undermine the power of influence because of the lack of recognition. When you recognize the advantages and the misappropriation of it, you glean truths that propel you into the sphere of success. Influence and its advantage is the foundation upon which one is positioned to learn, grow and thrive. The misappropriation of it leaves room for those with ill intentions to take advantage of others. Let's look at it from this perspective.

A teacher is one who has a great deal of influence. He or she spends substantial time with students in order to teach them. In many cases the student looks up the teacher. The student believes that what the teacher is teaching is correct. The student takes what the teacher has taught them and moves to the next level. None of this can be done without influence.

The flip side is when influence is misappropriated; people are mishandled and are often abused. Using the same scenario, instead of the teacher who holds that power using it in a positive light, you have those unfortunate situations when the influenced is used to do things we often see in the news or like Jonestown itself.

## THE INFLUENCE ON CULTURE

Have you ever wondered why trends come and go? Or perhaps why fashion changes at a rapid pace? It's clear, the turnover rate of the two is due to the influence on culture. Cultural influences have an effect on how we exist in marriage, how we raise our kids, our work ethic, and what type of music is dominating the airways.

Hip-Hop is a genre of music that has a great deal of influence. Hip-hop music is alleged to have been pioneered in New York's South Bronx in the mid 1970s by Jamaican-born Kool DJ Herc. At a Halloween dance party thrown by his younger sister, Herc used an innovative turntable technique to stretch a song's drum break by playing the break portion of two identical records consecutively. The popularity of the extended break lent its name to "breakdancing" a style specific to hip-hop culture, which was facilitated by extended drum breaks played by DJs at New York dance parties. It was at this moment that DJ Grandmaster Flash, Afrika Bambaataa, and Herc dominated New York's hip-hop scene. The rappers of Sugarhill Gang produced hip-hop's first commercially successful hit, "Rapper's Delight," in 1979.

Rap music was a combination of poetry and rhymes spoken over music that relied on the DJ's ability to work the turntables. What was thought to be just a African American hobby, later turned genre of music, began to explode throughout the country and by the 1980s there was no way you could ignore that hip hop was dominating as a movement. It was more than DJs with "skillz". It was more than a hot MC with the hottest song. It was more than music itself.

We saw under the auspice of President Ronald Reagan the 1980s fueled with racial injustice in the inner cities; social disparately among minorities coupled with an economy that did not favor anyone except the nation's elite. Hip-hop transended to become the voice for the people, Hip-hop became a force. In 1982, Grandmaster Flash would take the current state of inner cities that were plagued and write "The Message".

## *THE MESSAGE (LYRICS)*

*It's like a jungle sometimes it makes me wonder how I keep from going under. It's like a jungle sometimes it makes me wonder how I keep from going under*

*Broken glass everywhere  People pissing on the stairs, you know they just don't care  I can't take the smell, I can't take the noise no more  Got no money to move out, I guess I got no choice  Rats in the front room, cockroaches in the back  Junkie's in the alley with a baseball bat  I tried to get away, but I couldn't get far  'Cause a man with a tow-truck repossessed my car*

*Chorus: Don't push me cause I'm close to the edge  I'm trying not to lose my head, ah huh-huh-huh  It's like a jungle sometimes it makes me wonder how I keep from going under. It's like a jungle sometimes it makes me wonder how I keep from going under...*

This was also a time that other legendary artist would hit the scene with groundbreaking music such as The Fatback Band, Lady B, and Kurtis Blow. You had other greats come along such as Run DMC and of course the godfather of Hip-hop and co-founder of Def Jam Records, Russell Simmons. Hip-hop in its own right accelerated into a social machine that had an influence on culture that has just now garnered rightful recognition. We saw Hip-hop grow like a child from infancy stages to the trouble teens, all the way to adulthood.

You see, the late 70s - 80s was the time when Hip-hop, like a child, established foundation. There was a message and a cause. The 90s on the other hand were the times when rap became the run-away teen and succumbed to the message the previous generation had fought against. By this time, Hip-hop was about drugs, sex, gangs, and violence. The culture by the 90s had disintegrated to almost nothing. All that had been noticed was the east coast and west coast drama that left two icons, Tupac and B.I.G, dead without reason or explanation. Later, when we entered the 21$^{st}$ century, Hip-hop began to mature into adulthood accepting responsibility and shifting focus back to the issues of the day, all of which dramatically had an undeniable influence on our society.

## SOUND & HEARING

Sound as any musician will tell you has an enormous amount of power. It comes of no surprise that scientist have discovered just how powerful it can be with amplified volume from objects bouncing into air to the shattering of glass. Studies have shown that sound alone can even produce energy, create weapons, and even destroy weapons.

I read that researchers at the University of Arizona College of Engineering have come up with a novel way to help the U.S. Air Force dispose of stockpiles of dangerous chemicals using nothing more than sound waves.

The article went on to say that the U. S. Air Force has a large stockpile of almost 11 million liters of fire-extinguishing foam, which contains environmentally damaging organic compounds. Manish Keswani, an assistant professor in the department of materials science and engineering, and Reyes Sierra, a professor in the department of chemical and environmental engineering, have been awarded a $243,000 contract by the Air Force Civil Engineering Center to destroy the chemicals using a sonochemical process, which uses sound waves to break down complex and toxic molecules into nothing more than carbon dioxide and water.

The influence of sound alone has the ability to break down toxic molecules. Sound is necessary for us to understand the world that we live in. The Arnstending Institute held that "the most important aspects of sound are those qualities which convey emotions". In fact, the emotional qualities we do experience and become familiar with are caused mostly by sound. The extremely wide range of emotional gradations with which most of us are conversant could not have become known to us through first-hand, personal experience. For that, life is too short.

It is through the different expressive qualities of sound that we learn the various nuances and subtleties of emotion. This range of gradations in our emotional experience is communicated most often through the sonic forms, thereby saving us the need to have corresponding real-life experiences". With this revelation, I want to deal with your hearing and why it's important to manage what you let into your ear gate.

What you listen to and who you are listening to will shape your thoughts. Listening to greatness will eventually make you great. Listening to idiots will make you a fool. Your thoughts are what control your actions. Hearing the wrong things will cause you to make the wrong decisions and hearing the right things will cause you to make the right decisions.

Here is a good time for me to ask you some questions. What are you listening to? Are you listening to things that will cause you to be better? Or do you prefer to listen to things that have no reproductive abilities such as gossip. Are your ears being filled with information and spiritual food?

Who are you listening to? This is critical and not everyone understands this. Every winner should have a counsel of individuals who are qualified to speak to and advise them. These individuals hold the keys to your winning success. They have acquired knowledge and wisdom through experience to advise you. Choose these persons wisely. Be aware of those who attempt to make themselves this voice of reasoning in your life. They usually have an agenda.

The voice of a mentor, father or mother like person is your leader. It is the sound of their voice that summons your undivided attention. That sound you must acknowledge, honor, and cherish. '

## THE ABILITY TO PERSUADE

How do you get someone to believe in your dream? How do you get someone to invest in your idea? How do you convince someone that your plan is sure? It's called the ability to persuade. The main component to having influence is having the ability to persuade people. You can have a master plan but if you don't have what I've hailed "the gift", your plan is as good the paper it is written on. You must be able to convince others that you are good stock with low risk and the product you have to offer, the world cannot live without.

Your dream isn't some allusion that you happened to conjure up. Your dream is your life and trying to live without pursuing it with every fiber of your being means your not living. If you are actively in pursuit of your dream and you want to know how to get others to buy in, the first thing you must do is read code one if you haven't already. In that code I show you line upon line and precept upon precept how to first believe in yourself and believe in what you have to offer.

The second thing is to develop "the gift". In developing the gift to persuade, you must be able to understand your vision. For instance, you may have a vision to help people who are less fortunate. To properly understand your vision, you have to determine how you're going to help the less fortunate in a specific role and capacity. Once you know exactly how you're going to be of assistance, you can precisely communicate that.

Third, when you are developing the gift, you're going to need to build a following. Being able to build a following in your organization is important when you are working on innovation and dealing with the market in which you wish to exist. This following starts with your core group of people who see your idea just as you do. This core then seeks to establish the foundation of the idea. Once the foundation has been established, the idea has a purpose, goal, and mission, your core team will then illicit the opportunity for committed people to be a part.

Finally, your followers must understand the culture of your innovation. You just don't want others to simply go along for the ride. For example, you have two coffee houses and both have specialty coffee. One is corporately larger and the other is a smaller start up franchise.

The larger is known to have a café style setting with a dim light ambiance and the smaller franchise has very little seating at all and has brighter lights. The larger corporate structure offers more of a variety of coffee as well as other refreshments while the smaller doesn't have much of a selection at all.

Out of the two coffee houses, the larger is more prone to have a more structural culture that would require employees to be knowledgeable, trained, and vested in the business. This coffee house would be more demographically placed with a target audience.

The smaller coffee shop would be a slower pace environment that doesn't require its followers or employees to be as knowledgeable about the product or doesn't cater to the customers' need for a relaxed environment. The two have the same mission, which is to sell coffee, but they are culturally different. Your followers have to know the environment in which the idea and they themselves must exist in to effectively accomplish the overall mission.

If you neglect to persuade your followers, you must accept the fate of your failure. Although failure is optional and not a permanent place, you can avoid it by simply working "the gift".

## ATTRACTION

I cannot end this code without sharing this unique story as it relates to the law of attraction. There is much that I can say about this particular law. Many have written and shared important insights on this subject.

Some of the noteworthy insights you would hear are, "the more you focus on something the more powerful it becomes." Ester and Jerry Hicks describe this law which allows you to create your own reality by attracting the experiences you want.

Another law of attraction commonly known is, "like attracts like." This law varies and one definition of this particular one suggests that who you are is what you will attract. If you are negative, you will attract negativity. If you are positive, you will attract positive results.

While hanging out with my father one day, I realized that I had business to do at my bank. My father was in the driver seat while I was riding shotgun. Almost forgetting about the bank run, I stated to my dad with urgency that I needed to go the bank right away. My dad stated that he needed to make one stop on the way which was going towards the same direction.

After leaving were he needed to go, we headed to the bank. Here is what gave me great revelation. When we approached the bank and pulled into the parking lot, I noticed that my dad drove past the parking section and past the front door. Before I could ask him where he was going, he parked next to a tree that was situated on private property. There is a house that sits next door to my bank and the only thing that separates the two is grass and concrete.

When my dad drove in next to the tree, he put the car in park. He gets out of the car and start pulling off fruit. First of all, I'm livid because I know that this was someone's tree he's pulling from. Second of all, I'm confused as to how he knew that there was even a fruit tree there. I yell out the car to him to tell him that he knows better than to be picking fruit off a tree that belongs to someone else and then to tell him to come on.

When he gets back into the car with a bright smile and a handful of fruit, I asked him how did he know that was a fruit tree. What he said caused me to rethink the law of attraction. He replied, "I noticed the tree from way back there". Curious I asked, "way back where?" He said that he noticed the tree from the road before we turned into the parking lot.

The tree did not look like it had much of anything to me. It certainly did not look like it was full of apples. After thinking about this short and weird experience, it was clear to me that although the tree was full and productive, I wasn't attracted to it, partly due to the fact that I don't like apples. On the other hand, my dad just so happened to love apples and was attracted to the tree from afar.

You may have heard that "you shall know the tree by the fruit that it bares". This was especially the case. I love fruit, in particular, pears and peaches. I love different kinds of oranges and grapefruits. The question I want to pose for the winner is, what if a tree bares fruit that's not your particular fruit of choice? Clearly the tree is still productive but, how can you benefit from a tree that produce something you are not attracted to or perhaps isn't your particular flavor?

The great thing about the law of attraction that I learned first hand is this; just because something is productive and attractive to someone else doesn't necessarily mean it's for you. What attracts others may not be your flavor and may not even be of benefit to you. Find out what attracts you so that you can eat from that tree and gain resources. My father noticed the tree from a far distance due to this law, whereas I didn't even recognize the tree at all. What attracts you, you will immediately recognize.

## PEOPLE WHO INFLUENCE ME

In Business:

**Mark Elliot Zuckerberg** born May 14, 1984 is an American computer programmer, Internet entrepreneur, and philanthropist. He is best known as one of five co-founders of the social networking website Facebook. As of April 2013, Zuckerberg is the chairman and chief executive of Facebook, Inc. and his personal wealth, as of March 2014, is estimated to be $28.5 billion. His one-dollar salary puts him in the elite group of $1 CEOs.

Together with his college roommates and fellow Harvard University students Eduardo Saverin, Andrew McCollum, Dustin Moscovitz, and Chris Hughes, Zuckerberg launched Facebook from Harvard's dormitory rooms. The group then introduced Facebook onto other campuses nationwide and moved to Palo Alto, California shortly afterwards. In 2007, at the age of 23, Zuckerberg became a billionaire as a result of Facebook's success.

*- Wikipedia*


In Ministry & Business:

**Thomas Dexter Jakes Sr.** Bishop T. D. Jakes is a charismatic leader, visionary, provocative thinker, and entrepreneur who serves as senior pastor of The Potter's

House, a global humanitarian organization and 30,000-member church located in Dallas. Named "America's Best Preacher" by Time Magazine, Jakes' voice reverberates from the world's most prominent stages. Through his nexus of charitable works, T.D. Jakes is known for extending a hand of help to the needy, heart of compassion to the hurting, and message of inspiration to the disenfranchised. Beyond the pulpit, Jakes ranks among EBONY's Power100 and is the winner of several prestigious awards including BET Honors, Stellar Award, NAACP Image Award, Keeper of the Dream Award and McDonald's 365Black Award for his humanitarian efforts. His worldwide impact is also felt through high profile conference series such as MegaFest which recently drew more than 75,000 participants and an empire that spans film, television, radio, best-selling books, and the T.D. Jakes School of Leadership. Bishop Jakes made his presence felt in Hollywood with eight films to date including the recent hit, "Winnie Mandela" starring Jennifer Hudson; last year's top five release, "SPARKLE," featuring Jordin Sparks and the late Whitney Houston; "On the Seventh Day," the first sequel in the "Woman Thou Art Loosed" franchise which outperformed the competition on a per screen average; and "Jumping the Broom," an award winning romantic comedy that debuted as the #1 comedy and grossed nearly seven times its budget in 2011.

*Tdjakes.org*

Historically:

**Nelson Mandela** was born Rolihlahla Mandela on July 18, 1918. He grew up poor in a small South African village. When Mandela was nine, he was adopted by and sent to live with his father's friend, a prosperous clan chief. In school, Mandela learned about African history and his ancestors' struggles with discrimination. He wanted to help his countrymen. He later traveled to Johannesburg, where he studied law and opened the country's first black law practice. He also joined the African National Congress, a group that fought for racial equality.

In 1948, the government introduced apartheid, which left the country's nonwhite majority with few economic opportunities. In response, Mandela traveled throughout South Africa and encouraged people to take part in nonviolent demonstrations against the government's racial segregation policies. He was arrested for organizing anti-government activities and eventually sentenced to life in prison. "I have cherished the ideal of a democratic and free society in which all persons live together in harmony and with equal opportunities," he said during his trial. "It is an ideal which I hope to live for and to achieve. But if needs be, it is an ideal for which I am prepared to die."

Mandela's imprisonment led to protests around the world and economic sanctions, or limits on trade, against his country.

**First Black President** - On February 11, 1990, South African president F.W. de Klerk released Mandela from prison, and the two worked together to end apartheid. Three years later, they won the Nobel Peace Prize for their efforts.

In 1994, for the first time in South African history, nonwhites were allowed to vote in democratic elections. Mandela was elected president by an overwhelming majority. While in office, he worked to improve housing, education, and economic opportunities for the country's large black population. Mandela stepped down as president in 1999. That same year, he created the Nelson Mandela's Children Fund, a charity that helps poor South African children. "Children are the wealth of our country," he said in an interview with TFK in 2002. "They must be given love."

*-Time*

Musically:

**John Legend** The Ohio native and University of Pennsylvania graduate rocketed to stardom with his Columbia debut Get Lifted. The 2004 platinum set scored eight Grammy Award nominations for the former session player and vocalist (backing Lauryn Hill, Alicia Keys, Jay-Z, and Kanye West). Legend later won the first three of his nine Grammys: best new artist, best R&B album and best male R&B vocal performance for the hit single "Ordinary People." Two years later came his second platinum album, Once Again, with the Grammy-winning single "Heaven." Legend snared his third consecutive top 10 album with 2008's Evolver, spinning off the hit "Green Light" featuring Andre 3000.

John Legend has revealed several personas during his award-winning career. Singer/Songwriter. Musician. Producer. Philanthropist. Entrepreneur. To quote music industry pioneer Quincy Jones, the nine-time Grammy winner is simply "a genius." Writing about Legend for Time's 2009 tally of the 100 most influential people, Jones noted, "We've seen only the tip of the iceberg. For what he has already achieved in his career, it is going to be fun watching where he goes from here." The fun begins now. Legend, one of the industry's most innovative artists, returns after five years with his much-anticipated fourth solo album, Love in the Future (G.O.O.D/Columbia). Taking R&B/soul to the next level, Legend creates an immersive experience about romance, love, hope, commitment and optimism. Enhancing the experience: a rich, melodic soundscape--accented by compelling interludes--that fully integrates the musician's gospel and pop influences, classical training and unerring hip-hop/soul sensibilities.

*-Johnlegend.com*

Politically:

**Barack H. Obama** is the 44th President of the United States. His story is the American story — values from the heartland, a middle-class upbringing in a strong family, hard work and education as the means of getting ahead, and the conviction that a life so blessed should be lived in service to others.

With a father from Kenya and a mother from Kansas, President Obama was born in Hawaii on August 4, 1961. He was raised with help from his grandfather, who served in Patton's army, and his grandmother, who worked her way up from the secretarial pool to middle management at a bank.

After working his way through college with the help of scholarships and student loans, President Obama moved to Chicago, where he worked with a group of churches to help rebuild communities devastated by the closure of local steel plants. He went on to attend law school, where he became the first African-American president of the *Harvard Law Review*. Upon graduation, he returned to Chicago to help lead a voter registration drive, teach constitutional law at the University of Chicago, and remain active in his community.

President Obama's years of public service are based around his unwavering belief in the ability to unite people around a politics of purpose. In the Illinois State Senate, he passed the first major ethics reform in 25 years, cut taxes for working families, and expanded health care for children and their parents. As a United States Senator, he reached across the aisle to pass groundbreaking lobbying reform, lock up the world's most dangerous weapons, and bring transparency to government by putting federal spending online.

*-Whitehouse.gov*

# CODE FIVE

# SIGHT VS. VISION

*The only thing worse than being blind is having sight but no vision*

*-Helen Keller*

You may have heard in times past, believe half of what you hear and none of what you see. I endorse this philosophy, for the perils of eyesight will often lead to deception. Not long ago I vacationed in Disney in Orlando, Florida. While there I visited the Epcot theme park, you know, the one with the gigantic iconic spaceship earth at the entrance. I was amazed at what my eyes saw as I perused the different attractions, all of which were very educational. So I decided to get on this particular ride and what I heard struck a nerve. "What we see limits the eyes of our imagination." Let's talk about the difference of sight vs. vision.

A winner should never make a single decision based

on mere sight without information. Once all data necessary has been gathered and analyzed, a conscious decision is made based on the ability to see the outcome from the start. This is vision and it is the same system that God used when creating the universe.

In the process of creation, what the Creator saw was total darkness. But His vision; the eyes of His imagination saw Jupiter, Pluto, and even Earth. Because of the mass darkness, He knew that in order to actually see, He had to think of something to solve the problem. So He imagined the sun so that there would be daylight and the moon for lighting at night. God even imagined you.

You too may be looking with your natural eyes and all that you see is darkness. The truth is, everything you want out of life exists inside that darkness. It is up to you to turn on the light and envision every detail. If your sight lead you alone, then you will become overwhelmed with the fear I described in the third code. You will be afraid of the dark.

I remember as a child playing the "are you afraid of the dark?" game. I'm not sure that it's an actual game but it's something I did with siblings and cousins. The gist of game was to walk in a dark room and shut the door until you couldn't take it anymore. The psychology of it was that you stand in the dark long enough until your mind would make you think that something was going to get you. Because you could not physically see, you believed it.

Like a child, most people in adolescent stages are afraid to enter into a place. That place may or may not be familiar but, because it's dark, fear takes over. Great things often come out of dark places. In the 19th century prior to modern technology, Polaroid and Kodak spearheaded a method to develop film. This was the darkroom method and the only way you could get a good image printed was in using this method. A darkroom is a room that is made completely dark for the processing of light sensitive photographic materials. Those materials then go through a process of development.

Consider for a moment that your brainchild is one that is light sensitive. Consider that it cannot be prematurely exposed to others who lack capacity to handle such a big deal in a small beginning. In order for it to go through the development process, it must sit for a period of time in a dark place. Why abort that child because you cannot see in the place that was designed for it to evolve?

Perhaps other areas of your life are in a dark place such as your marriage, finances, career or your family. Just because you cannot see the solutions doesn't mean that they aren't there. Allow your situation to remain in the darkroom until it's fully developed. Put your vision spectacles on and see what it will be after it comes out of the darkroom.

Sight alone will never be in the welfare of a winner. Sight permits you to peruse, observe, and inquire. But sight does not afford you the luxury to see beyond natural limitations. It makes you aware, but it doesn't make you understand. Sight gives you a visual, but it doesn't promise a vision. It is because of this that I began this code with that quote.

Helen Keller started out a normal infant who cried, recognized sounds, objects, and murmured like any normal child for the first two years of her life. Then suddenly she was struck with an illness said to be scarlet fever. Although the illness did not last long, it took away her ability not just to see and hear, but also to speak.

Life for her after, from childhood to an adult, became a story of victory over devastation and crippling affliction. In time, Helen learned to "see" past her blindness, deafness, and muteness; she could "see" and "hear" with exceptional keenness. She even learned to speak fairly. Over a span of time, Ms. Keller graduated college, became a writer and humanitarian. In her later years a reporter asked her, what could possibly be worst than being blind? she replied: to have sight and no vision.

Understand, how then vision superseded the bottomless pit of sight. Ms. Keller could have allowed her natural limitation to prevent her from making a major impact. She could have retreated to some sort of disability community to reside with others with like disabilities. But rather than to do so, she chose to follow purpose regardless of what sought to limit her.

Doctors have come up with a unique way of determining what is "normal" vision. They determine what is normal based on the Snellen chart created in 1862 by Dutch ophthalmologist Herman Snellen. You will be most familiar with this if you have ever visited an eye doctor and or wear prescription glasses. According to this chart, there is a break down from letters to numbers that display on the chart. The lines upon which the letters are displayed calculate distance and the numbers calculate the sharpness of your sight. I want to focus your attention on a few of them.

Let's talk first about 20/20 vision. I want to caution you that although this medical term uses the word "vision", it's actually referring to eyesight. This particular vision is what is defined as standard or normal and it is rated based on comparison with other individuals. If you are person with 20/20 vision, it means when you stand twenty feet away from the Snelling chart you can see what normal people can see. The problem I have with this is that the formula within itself seeks to define how well you see based on another's ability. It places you on the same level as someone else.

So then the question is, do you want to see what others see? Or, do you see something far beyond? As a visionary, you are supposed to be an innovator discovering new concepts, new processes, and perhaps even showing old dogs new tricks. If you are seeing on the same level, how is this possible? Hear me, you do not in any way want to be on the same level as anyone. It's not cool at all to be normal nor has it ever been. What's in you requires you to see what others have never seen.

Then there is 20/10 vision. This is defined as better than normal vision and it means that a person can see twenty feet away what others can see ten feet away. If you are a person with 20/10 vision, your able to gauge possible opportunities much sooner than a person of the opposite. How far you can see at less of a distance will give you a head start. This is extremely important if you plan to be competitive in any market.

## EAGLE VISION. BUZZARD SIGHT.

Eagles are an unique species and there are more than sixty kinds of eagles in the world. The most common are the bald eagle and golden eagle. What interests me the most about this bird is its sharp vision. Researchers have speculated that the vision of an eagle is somewhere around 20/2. In comparison to any bird of it's kind with the exception of one, that being a crow, the eagle is the smartest and most precise bird.

Eagles are large powerfully built birds of prey. Its body structure is massive yielding a heavy head and beak. Like all birds of prey eagles have large hooked beaks for tearing flesh from their prey, strong legs and power claws to grip and carry its prey. Eagles can have a wingspan of seven feet, and be up to three and half feet tall. It can also have the adult weight of over fifty pounds.

Eagles usually build their nest in tall trees or on high cliffs. These nests are called eyries. Very seldom will you find an eagle near surface level, as it is not in their nature. All of their dealings are most likely to happen from high in the air. These are high altitude beings that only comprehend living from that viewpoint.

Because eagles are species of prey, it's not usual for them to feed on things that are already dead. In fact the reason they are called species of prey is because they catch there meals alive, kill them, and then eat. Most eagles can grab their prey without landing and take flight with it to be carried and prepared for dinner at another location. The bald eagle has been noted to carry a live mule deer with an average weight of one hundred and fifty pounds as prey.

What is most powerful about an eagle is not there muscular body or the width span of their wings. It's not the different variations of an eagle. Neither is it their appetite for things that are living although these are important things not to neglect. I will show you later how they are applicable. The most powerful thing about an eagle is their binocular vision.

The word binocular comes from the root word *bini*, which means double, and *oculus*, which means eye. Having two eyes that are simultaneous would have the advantage of four. Let's explore these four. First, binocular vision gives a creature a spare set of eyes in case one set is damaged. Second, it gives the creature a wider view range. For instance, humans have a maximum horizontal field of view of approximately 190 degrees with two eyes. This is about 120 degrees of which makes up the binocular field of view (seen by both eyes), bordered by two uniocular fields (seen by only one eye) of approximately 40 degrees. Third, binocular vision gives the creature the ability to see enhanced minuscule objects. Fourth, it can give a creature exact depth perception.

Most animals that have eyes positioned on opposite sides of their head have to move their head along with moving their eyes independently in order two improve field of view. This is not the case for eagles. For creatures that prey other living animals such as an eagle usually have eyes positioned on the front of their head. This allows for the eagle to have binocular vision. Most importantly they have this view with out a single eye movement.

For humans there is a slight difference although we have eyes position on the front of our head. There is a technical term called binocular rivalry. When very different images are shown to the same retinal regions of the two eyes, perception settles on one for a few moments, then the other, for as long as one stares at the image. This is the alternation of perception between the images of the two eyes. So for humans we cannot have binocular vision in reality but we can have it in principle.

When the nature of an eagle is studied fully, you then understand the being they are and how they operate. Everything an eagle does is from a high perspective. They congregate in high places. They view the world from up high rather than below. They nest high up in the air. They see opportunities below from thousands of feet in the troposphere. They live by principle in their own right and there are things that they just won't do. This is a far contrast to large birds such as a buzzard.

All though a buzzard has fairly good vision, it does not rely on its vision as seeing is not as important. A buzzard will rely on other senses mainly their extraordinary sense of smell. It prefers the sense of smell to detect things that are lifeless, rotting, and stinking. Buzzards have a difficult time seeing in the dark and will only go about its routine during the day. A buzzard doesn't normally wake up before 9 a.m. You will usually see them gathered in flocks.

If you notice a flock of buzzards gathered in one place, it will most likely be in rural areas, in or near roadways, or even landfills. This often signals that a dead animal is in the vicinity. Buzzards eat road kill-the carcasses of animals that were hit by cars. Buzzards are not picky eaters and will eat just about any dead animal such as possums, squirrels, rabbits, deer, domestic animals and even skunks (although they will leave the scent pouch of a skunk intact). When buzzards have a choice between fresh road kill and a decayed animal carcass, they will always choose the fresh kill.

In comparison, we have two large birds with good "vision". One is up early in the morning and the other gets up later in the morning. One soars high and the other rides the heat currents never really exerting itself. One relies on vision and the other relies on smell. One prefers to feed on things that are alive while the other wants things that are dead. One travels alone and the other always has like-minded birds with them.

Here is why this portion of the code is vital. You have to determine whether or not you have eagle vision or buzzard sight. Have you ever noticed people who always have a pack of other people with them? Have you ever noticed when having encountered those people that they never have anything thing good to say about anybody? And if caught alone they will even talk about the very ones they hang with?

I called this particular group the buzzard pack. This pack will never reveal the positive things about others or perhaps how the very ones they speak negatively about has helped them in some way. This group of people always feed on gossip, rumors and other trash. They fly at low altitudes never aiming or actively working to achieve anything higher in life. They are essentially low lives.

Those with eagle vision are what I call champions. These individuals very seldom hang or travel in packs but understand the necessity of having a vision inspired team. Champions only feed on things that have life, which has the ability to reproduce, never being reduced to gossip and rumors. These select groups of people have binocular vision in principle, being able to gauge and detect minute opportunities from a high perspective. Champions never have time for anything other than progress, for it is not enough to have 20/20, 20/10, or 20/2 visions.

## WHAT DO YOU SEE?

A remarkable story took place in the scriptures particularly in the New Testament and it is one regarding Jesus' encounter with a certain blind man. There are several cases in which Jesus performed similar miracles for those who were blind. I believe this particular one is set apart as it reveals a hidden truth.

After Jesus fed the multitudes that followed him and sent them home, he and his disciples set out to journey to another place. When they arrived at a place called Bethsaida, a blind man was brought to Jesus by those who lived there and asked if he could restore the blind man's sight. We don't know much about this man as the scriptures doesn't so much as give us his name. Jesus then took him by the hand and led him out of what was most familiar to him (his village). Then he does something that is unorthodox to human comprehension and put saliva in the blind man's eyes. Afterwards he asks the blind man, what do you see?

When then blind man opens his eyes, he responds to the question with "I see men that look like trees walking". Ironically in the Old Testament of scripture is a situation in the first chapter of Psalms. This situation deals with stipulated blessings or cause and effect blessings. One promise of the blessing was that those who met the stipulations would be like a tree firmly planted. Fast-forward to this blind man's miracle, he saw that those who were planted now walking.

This would be a good arguing point. I want to believe that the whole miracle that Jesus performed with this blind man really had nothing to do with just eyesight. I believe that Jesus wanted him to have more than sight. Jesus gave this man vision. When the blind man received his sight, he revealed something that took place thousands of year's prior. What the man revealed who now has sight and vision was that we were no longer planted under stipulated blessings. We are in fact walking in the blessing.

For the winner, this is not the time to walk by sight. This is the time to walk by the faith I shared in code three. The kind of faith that has a vision of something that no one ever imagined you could do. The kind of faith that has binocular vision. The faith that assures you that you're walking in the blessing no matter what your eyes tell you.

*Never take advice from failing people - Guy Reeves Jr.*

There is another winners law I want to give you. This is what I've dubbed "the blind led effect". It is a common thing when you see those who are blind with a guide dog. A guide dog is dog trained to assist by leading blind and visually impaired people. A guide dog goes through a series of training sessions to recognize sounds, commands and navigation around obstacles. The primary job of a guide dog is to ensure that the person it's leading gets to their destination. They also assist in finding things such as personal items, chairs, and destinations by name. Though it sounds simple, the skill and attention to detail is key. After graduating training school, they are highly sophisticated and qualified to handle such a task.

The challenge with having a guide dog is that the dog itself is colorblind. With all of its acquired knowledge and learned instinct, the dog will not be able to recognize signs. Because it will not be able to recognize signs, the guide dog has that margin of error. For example, the dog has the task of leading it's master across the street where a stop sign is located. If for one second the dog has forgotten key elements in training, it can cause a fatal accident between itself, his master, and automobile.

This is essentially what happens when blind people in principle lead other blind people. There is a passage of scripture found in the synoptic gospels that says, "if the blind lead the blind, they both fall into a pit". It is so easy to follow those who you think have your answers. What I've discovered is that it's more common with family, however, it exists everywhere.

The tragedy of following someone who is not trained and qualified to lead you will ultimately lead you deeper into a ditch than you were before, in part, because they cannot recognize the warning signs…signs that say "dead end" or signs that say "stop". Like a guide dog, they have limited abilities.

Winners have mentors. A mentor is a trusted advisor with proven results of winning in the particular area in which you desire to excel. If you want to excel in the medical field as a doctor, after completing your studies you have to go through a residency program. Being a resident doctor ensures that you are advised and monitored for the best possible results by a more experienced chief physician. It would be ridiculous for a resident doctor to be advised by a medical assistance or perhaps even a licensed practitioner nurse. They are not on the same level of expertise.

If you set out to win, you must follow someone who has already been where you want to go. Just because they're your "roadies" doesn't mean they are qualified to advise you. Just because it's your mother or father doesn't necessarily mean they are able to lead you beyond a certain point of your life. You must seek out someone who isn't blind or easily blind-sided. They must have vision. Maybe you are reading this and your wondering how to stop following the blind. Here are two simplistic ways to do so.

1. Stop taking advice from failing people. A good friend of mine who I quoted shared this advice with me years ago. If a person is failing, how can they give you advice? How can someone who is poor teach you how to get wealth if they themselves have never been wealthy? How can someone lead you through the maze of life and they are still stuck in the maze? Don't be ridiculous.

For many of you who are reading this, I must forewarn you that when you stop excepting everyone's advice, you will gain enemies. You will be accused of thinking that you know it all. Don't let that stop you from putting priority to that relationship and if it's real, they will understand.

2. Find five people who are already doing what you want to do and pattern yourself after them. Some you do not have to personally know. You need at least one mentor who is accessible. I've done the same and I took the initiative to list some of my influencers in code four.

Last, is x-ray vision. This particular vision enables the winner to see above "see level" or beyond the surface. The official definition of x-ray vision is the ability to see through objects. I am confident that on your journey, you're going to need this ability to see through circumstances, situations and even people.

There will be times in your life, if you haven't experienced it already, when everything about your world will be in a dark place. It will seem as though everything is in disarray and you cannot see anything. You will not be able to see a way out of tough times. You will come face to face with fear and doubt.

This is when having x-ray vision, the supernatural ability to see your way through, will be your greatest strength. That strength is knowing who's holding your hand while walking through those valleys of shadows of death.

You will need to employ the same vision to see past people. People will always be people. They will always be unpredictable. Some people will never change. See right through them and move on.

# CODE SIX

# ARGUE THE POINT

It was the summer of 2000 and I just reached the legal working age. Back then my uncle would allow me to work for him at his furniture store during the summer months. There was not one soul within a forty-mile radius of Wilmington who did not shop at or know of Reeves Used Furniture, a family owned and operated business. This is a well known and well to do family with roots tied deeply in ministry. It was there that I learned my work ethic.

Most nights I'd spend the night at his house. This was common because his son and I are cousins and best friends, even today. Our usual morning would consist of my uncle coming in the room to wake us up. This was not an easy thing because we'd stay up late most nights. He would come in the room and with a soft yet commanding voice, we would hear, "Booper and Stadus, let's go boys". Booper was his nickname for my cousin.

My name has always been difficult for those in my family to pronounce, "Stadus " was one of many that I became accustomed to. We would reluctantly get up, shower and dress.

My uncle had such a discipline and work ethic that I never saw. He would already be up around 6 am in the morning drinking coffee and reading the newspaper. He didn't watch much TV but he still relied on the radio to get local and national news. My uncle is what we call old school. By the time my cousin and myself would be dressed and ready, he would already be waiting in his pick up truck.

After we'd get in the truck, the first order of business would be morning runs. The first stop was always the bank run. He always did his bank run early in the mornings; traits that I learned from him and still do till this day. After the bank, the next stop was the Krispy Krème or Dunkin' Donuts and then off to the store. Occasionally we picked up furniture from a wholesaler.

My uncle is a man that is no more than five feet, six inches tall and medium build. Then he was in his late fifties and what was mind boggling to me was his enormous strength. Once we would get to the store that was situated in a strip mall, the task of pulling the large appliances such as refrigerators, stoves, washer machines, and dryers out for display began. I watched in amazement of how he moved heavy furniture often times without using a lift dolly. He is not your typical elderly man.

My uncle, affectionately known as Mr. Reeves, but is Uncle Guy to me, is the lovable community guy. His heart for people would cause him to go above and beyond for those that needed his business services but may not have had financial means to acquire what they came to the store to buy. I've personally seen this man literally give away hundreds if not thousands of dollars in merchandise away without breaking a sweat to single parent families or just the average guy who would come. If Uncle Guy had a clue that you were in need, he would make a way. At times I would wonder if the business was a charity or if it was actually a store. Interestingly enough, it was a very prosperous and profitable business.

Then there were those moments when people would come in not to buy anything but to talk to Mr. Reeves. He had a way of listening to people, even to the locals who's norm was to be intoxicated. People would come in from all backgrounds to discuss a variety of issues from business, to current affairs, personal issues and even ministry related things.

My days consisted of answering phones, talking to customers, both of which help me learn people skills and the art of negotiation. Moving furniture in and out of both the store and the storage unit where the stock inventory was kept. On the weekends, Uncle Guy would allow my cousin and I to take select merchandise to the local farmers market where we were allow to negotiate, sell, and keep the profits. As the businessman he is, he received his share. A third of our total earnings would go to him; after all it was his merchandise. All that I know about business is because of Uncle Guy. That experience was my foundation.

My father taught me how to work as a man. He always worked in corporate America and had supervisor positions with Fortune 500 companies such as Boeing. My uncle taught me how to work as hard more on the entrepreneurial side. My uncle taught me to be my own boss and to work for myself. Although both men made good money, one was my poor dad and the other was my rich dad, if we were to put it into Robert Kiyosaki's, author of *Rich Dad Poor Dad* terms.

As the summer came near to end, I knew that working for my uncle wouldn't be possible as I was soon on my way back to school. By the time I would get off of school, the store would be gearing up to close for the day. So I had to think of another means to make money. My parents demanded after a certain age that their children work and they would have it no other way…school or no school.

One day in late August of that year, I sat at Uncle Guy's desk at the store and grabbed phone sitting on top of the file cabinet. I opened it up to the law firm section and began dialing numbers. My cousin told me of positions that law offices usually have for teenagers after school. He and his friend previously worked for a firm. So I thought, let's give it a try.

I dialed one number after another to inquire if they were hiring a runner. A runner is someone that transported legal documents by foot from law firm to other law firms and courts. The position also consisted of depositing large sums of cash and checks into bank accounts. After daily runs were finished then you'd come back to the office and be an office assistant. As an office assistant your responsibility was answering phones, faxing, and copying.

After calling several law firms asking if they were hiring for that position, I hit the jackpot. The receptionist on the other end said yes, took my information, and set up a day and time for me to come in. This was my first interview and I was excited. This was my first official job prospect and at that point, I have never been on an interview before.

The day came that was scheduled for me to interview. I put on the best suit I had in my closet. Back then my best was a black polyester suit from the local Menswear store downtown. I took the city bus from where I lived to Wilmington's business district, which happens to be the credit card capital of the world. I get off at Rodney Square the former bus terminal and walk a block away to 824 N. Market Street.

I walk into the office building, sign in at the security desk and jump on the elevator. I pushed the button to go to the eighth floor and when I got off the elevator I was met with two glass doors with an elegantly situated sign over top that read; Agostini, Levitsky, Isaacs & Kulesza. I take a deep breath and walk in. At the entrance, the receptionist met me with a warm welcome and I introduced myself. As I sat waiting for the interview to began I recalled everything that my mother taught me. Most importantly, don't forget to use my manners. She was a stickler for yes ma'am, no ma'am, yes sir, no sir.

The receptionist received a call and afterwards she looked at me and said "Mr. Levitsky is ready to see you now". I was escorted to a large conference room elegantly situated where the meeting was to take place. I sit down and moments later a tall man walked in and introduce himself as Neal Levitsky. Immediately, I stand to greet him with a firm handshake just as my father taught me.

I didn't have a resume and the only other place I have ever worked was for my uncle. So he asked me to tell him a little about myself. I proceeded to tell him what little I could and afterwards he described all that the position required. He told me that there was something different about me and that he wanted me to fill the position. One stipulation was that whenever I did not have school, he wanted me to attend court with him as an assistant.

It would be a few weeks later before I started and on my first day I walk in with excitement that cannot be explained. My thoughts were, I landed a job and not just any job...I actually work for a law firm. Once again the receptionist greeted me but this time as an employee. She gives me a more in depth tour of the firm and eventually we ended up at what would be my desk. It was stationed next to the lead paralegal and once she gave me all of the information needed, she told me to sit down. I was given my own extension number and it was time to record my own voicemail. You have to remember, I was just a kid and this was my first official gig not to mention it's a two to three hour a day job after school.

I remember candidly my boss calling me into his office to ask for my progress report. He was very interested in my grades in school and insisted that education was the key to being successful. Within a few days I produced my report, which wasn't my best, but it was fair enough. He looked at it, gave his recommendation and asked when was the next time I had a full day off of school. When I told him he checked his schedule and told me that he wanted me to attend court with him on that day. He wanted me to dress appropriately; preferably in a suit and that I had to be in the office at by 9:00a.m. that morning.

I show up that morning dressed and ready, not sure what quite to expect. My boss comes out of his office to make sure I'm prepared to represent him and the firm.

He gives me my assignment for the day while in the courtroom and that was to do or say nothing. Just watch, listen, and maintain a good posture he said. So we head out for the courthouse.

Minutes later we arrive on foot and through the medal detectors we go. We go into the courtroom and wait for the judge to approach the bench. Ten minutes go by and in walks the judge but there is no jury. There are a group of lawyers on one side and there were the three of us on the other side. This all seemed odd to me but again my job was to do or say nothing, just watch. Proceedings began and all I could see was civilized arguing back in forth between that group of attorneys and our group. There was a lot of paper work and books.

My assessment of what was taking place in that courtroom was a matter of two sides arguing a point. The judge served as a mediator between the two parties. The files and law books served as a point of reference. Although I'm not sure to this day what actual proceeding was taking place, this was very alluring and I learned in my first court appearance a masterful strategy.

I've always believed that I had two callings, one was to be a minister and the other was to be a lawyer. One I pursued vigorously and the other I did not. As far as I can remember, my love for God, law, and politics has always been there. My case is one that leaned more towards faith-oriented endeavors. It seems my call to minister took precedence over the other and even still, my love for both remains.

The two callings have much in common. Both require ones ability to entertain and to effectively communicate a point. Both require extensive schooling in their respective fields and both demand the need for debate. It was during my first courtroom experience that I learned to debate. I call it arguing the point.

Communication in all aspects of life is essential. Nothing in the world operates to its fullest potential without meaningful communication and a part of communication is debating. I don't care how hard you try; you will not be able to avoid debating to some degree. Some people debate due to disagreements and others debate because they are fools. The key to properly debating with an intended resolve, requires information. Communication without information is a dead dialog. No one gets anywhere.

There is a purposeful way to debate and that is to argue the point for clarity and understanding. There is an unproductive way to debate and that's without having a solid reason, information, or an expected end. Arguing the point gets to the root of the matter. Notice I said matter and not problem, this is because every thing that is cause for debate is not always a problem. It could simply be an unresolved matter.

Arguing the point allows one side to offer a point during the course of a conversation. The other side then responds with a counter point. Once both sides get their point across in a way that can be received and understood, common ground is more easily obtainable. If the two sides cannot do so then there must be the opportunity to come back to the table for further communication. This will ensure that the matter is not ignored, hence evolving into a potential irreconcilable problem.

Case and point, boy meets girl. The two are attracted to each other and decide to date. Boy and girl are in a relationship with the challenge of two opposite upbringings. One has the proclivity to spend more money than what is actually coming in. The other is use to saving at least thirty percent of all income. The two come to the table to argue the point of saving. Boy and girl do not reach an agreement and promises to come back to the table. One has the responsibility of gathering tools and resources. Eventually they come back to the table to further argue the point. Boy and girl decide to save at least ten percent of all income and the matter is settled.

Something that caught my attention in that initial courtroom experience was that at times, the tone, action, and reaction modulated. The levels in the room went up and down as the arguments intensified. They were manageable levels and the judge was making sure of that.

After observing a while, it was very clear that this was normal for human nature. The point is this; never neglect a valid point because you don't like the tone in which it was given. The point must still be argued until there is an agreement.

Understand that both parties in that courtroom that day were obviously of a mature level. Their profession demanded that they had some level maturity but even with that, during the course of arguing the point, the judge had to chime in to make sure they stay true the core issue. Take this model and put it into every day life and you will see that sometimes while arguing the point you may need a mediator.

A mediator is a middle man or woman that makes sure the debate to resolve the matter stays true to the mainline issue at hand. Mediators never take sides and always stays neutral. Tensions may rise and emotions may go left but a good mediator is one who can defuse a situation. Mediators often act as peacemakers.

## BE IN THE KNOW

In order to win in the area of communication, you must be in the know. Being in the know means that you are constantly educating yourself. Not just on issues that most interest you but on a wide range of issues. Issues like world news, current affairs, or climate change. Being in the know puts you at greater risk of winning in the areas in which you wish to succeed. All things in some way or another have a connection and being in the know helps you to connect the dots.

For the winner who wants to communicate on another level and implement my strategy of arguing the point, being in the know is non-negotiable. Information is key and it allows you to have a point of reference. To debate without a point of reference will dilute your voice and those you communicate with will not value your voice, opinion, or point of view.

It wouldn't be smart to converse about finances and you know nothing about money. It wouldn't be smart to argue theology and you know nothing about God. If you have not educated yourself on those matters, you are not qualified to discuss those matters. The reason being, you have no point of reference. You have nothing to point to as a means to base your claim. If your argument has no foundation, you have no argument.

Let's use this scenario as an example but before we do, know that this can go both ways. If a woman decides to date a man and decides later on down the road that he isn't the right one, she has that right to do so. The challenge would be her reason of why he isn't the right one or what led her to that conclusion. Was he not a real man? Did he not maintain his responsibility? Was he not a go getter? What must be determined is who is her point of reference. Did she have a father or father figure in her life that maintained his responsibility? Was her father a go getter? Was her father a "real man"? If so, what constitute her father to be so?

If the woman making the decision that the man isn't the right one based on her criteria of a man and she's never had a father or figure alike in her life by which she can point to, then she has no valid reason to end it. Now if she didn't have a father figure but later on connected to a father-like mentor who possess all of the qualities that make up a good man, then she has a point of reference. She can point to a man by which she can base her reason.

## NEGOTIATE

It is true that most laws are created, amended, and argued based on previous related cases. Supreme court decisions are nothing more than justices arguing the point of law based on what set previous precedence to determine what's constitutional. If you ever want to gauge your next victory, simply remember the last the victory you won. Your last victory is your point of reference.

Arguing the point increases the ability to negotiate. Negotiation is a dialog between two or more people or parties with the intent to reach an understanding, settle a point of difference, and to draft contractual agreements that would be in the interest of both parties. Negotiation puts you in the driver seat as you drive on the road towards compromise.

Negotiation in its most common use is found in business, legal proceedings, churches, charities, parenting, marriage and divorce. It's even found in multiple levels government such as the job of Secretary of State and sometimes that of former Presidents like Jimmy Carter who spearhead peace talks. Negotiation is found in hostage situations where police find common ground with the perpetrator. Even so, the main ingredient is the ability to argue the point. An intricate part of winning on any level relies heavily on whether or not you can negotiate a deal.

A few years back while still serving as pastor of Champions Church, it was decided that we needed a permanent location to worship. So I sought out a few local buildings and came across a few storefronts. The congregation wasn't large in numbers and in fact we were a start up ministry. We didn't need to bite more than we could chew in terms of space but we did need room to grow.

In my search for the right location demographically, I came across the particular strip mall and decided that it was a great place to host a church. It was an unorthodox location but it was doable. I reached out to the property owners and asked for a meeting and they granted my request. We met at the actual location where the building was and I shared my vision of what I wanted to do. I was given a tour of the building and after we sat down to discuss logistics. At the end of our meeting I was given a lease application.

I gathered the team and took them to the hopeful location of our new church home. In all reality, there wasn't much there to see as the unit was just twelve hundred square feet. There was a small closet that would be the potential office and one restroom that would serve as a his and her restroom. The property owner allowed us to go in and as we walked, I shared vision in detail down to the carpet color, the wall color, and the culture of the new space. Optimism was in the air.

Shortly after, I sit down and looked at the four-page lease agreement and began filling it out. Afterwards I started thinking of ways to gather money for such a project. Once we had the finances required, I called the landlord to schedule a meeting to sign the lease. The day was set at October 4th, which was one week away. When that day came, I took two officials from the ministry to the lease signing.

When we met at the office that day, I knew that this was a great opportunity for me and the ministry however I didn't know in what way. I walk in the office with the two officials from the church as confident as I knew how. I was dressed in a three-piece suit and ready to do business. We sit down in the conference room and go over the lease and its terms and conditions. A lot was explained and much was not. But I didn't see anything alarming so I signed my John Hancock on the dotted line.

The problem was I knew nothing about commercial lease agreements. It hadn't dawned on me that residential and commercial lease agreements were like night and day. The only thing I knew was that by signing on the dotted line would guarantee our congregation access to a semi permanent home. As far as the legalities would be another issue I would soon come to know.

I signed the deal, handed them the cashier's check and inside I exploded with joy. I stood up and gave everyone a firm handshake and they handed me the key. The only part of the deal that I was able to negotiate was we were not to pay rent until we actually began having services in the facility. The fact that we were a non-profit organization seemed to have been in our favor. We were set to have our first champion experience in our new facility the first Sunday in January of that year. This gave us a three-month advantage of renovating the place to our liking.

The time came to celebrate the New Year and we were as ready as we were going to be. Then that day came, I remember it vividly because it was the day after Christmas. I get a phone call from the company that leased the property to us asking to meet with me asap. Of course, I said; after all they were very kind and gracious to us, accommodating us in any way they possibly could. The meeting was schedule for that next day and I show up. There I was met with warm greetings from the owners and when we sat down I got the news.

Sometime in early December, the company had sold the property to a larger real estate company. This was a well-known commercial company. They stated that they received an offer for the property that they could not refuse and reassured me that my existing contract wouldn't be affected. The look on my face must have given them the impression that I wasn't fond about what I was hearing. They proceeded to tell me that the official transition would take place January 1st.

I remember pausing for a few moments knowing that this has to some how affect us in a negative way. It was one of the things I knew in my knower. When I came to myself, I asked, "what's the next step?" The owners responded with, "the next step is to meet the new owners." I'm thinking, wow, Ok. I really like the way things were going with our relationship and I never would have imagined that it would end.

Nonetheless, I, along with the other tenants meet at the property with both companies. We listened in at what both parties had to say concerning the transition. There was a vibe in the room as the new company laid out plans that weren't pleasant. I particularly like certain changes that were slated to take place with the facelift of the building and the signage. The physical aspect of their vision would modernize the property making it more noticeable.

After the meeting they wanted to meet with each individual tenant and I was first. For a few brief minutes they shared that there was existing lease signed and that although a church was not in their plans for the property, they had to honor it. They stated that they had not looked at the lease as of yet but would so in the coming days. It was obvious that these guys were strictly business and was less favorable with non-profit organizations than the previous owners.

Before our meeting was adjourned I was given an ultimatum disguised in a suggestion to move a few units down upon which I respectfully declined. Clearly my existing lease was for the unit we had already prepared. At this point I knew that this situation would soon end and if not it was going to be a legal battle I wasn't prepared for. When I declined, they rebutted with strong consideration to do so. Now wait, pause. I love God and all that good stuff but I'm from "the hood". The notion that anyone is going to force my hand or get over on me is just ridiculous. So I stood up and in a "hood" way strongly reminded them that I already had a contract in place and walked out.

The reasoning behind the move was to accommodate other tenants that they drew up plans for. My issue was that the unit in which they wanted us to occupy had a seven-foot ceiling while my current unit had a ten-foot ceiling. There were plans to have stage lighting installed mid January. A seven-foot ceiling was not doable for us. The facts were, we already completed eighty percent of our renovation project.

Two weeks into hosting services in our new sanctuary I get another call. This call came directly from the gentlemen I had to confront and they wanted to meet. At that time, I was there having noonday prayer and stated to them that I was inside the unit and that we could meet that day. We set up a time to meet a few hours after that call. When they arrived we sat down and they began sharing that they were personally vested in the project and that they were two hundred thousand dollars in and that we were only a few thousand in. They reiterated their vision for the property and once again stated that a church wasn't a fit for their plans.

The one gentleman pulled out of his brief case a copy of the lease I signed with the previous owners. He went to a page, which stated that had certain clauses. One was that if the property was sold, the existing contract was legal and binding but certain terms of the lease could be amended under new owners. Highlighted was a clause that stated under new ownership, the rent could be modified to fit the terms and conditions of the new company.

By this point I know that my hands were tied so I look at them square in the eye and ask, what will the new monthly rent be? They responded by telling me that the rent for most of the tenants on the commercial side will go up and in my particular case it will go from twelve hundred and fifty dollars a month to almost sixteen hundred dollars a month. I thought you have to be kidding me. They went on to say that it was effective immediately and that a failure to sign a new lease with that change would automatically null and void the old existing lease. The problem with that was, the church would loose the deposit held in an escrow account.

I get up, shake hands with the gentlemen, get a copy of the new lease and told them I would get back to them. They said take your time and for the next few days I scrutinize the new lease agreement and prayed for direction. After reading and researching certain elements of the lease I felt led not to sign it. This was a difficult decision because I did not want to get the ministry jammed into another situation. On the same hand, what do I tell the people? Do I sign the lease or do I risk loosing it all?

I called the company back and asked for a meeting and so we met that day as we were both scheduled to be on location. When they arrived I gave them a blank contract and told them that it would be in the best interest of the ministry to count our losses. I could see the relief on their faces as clearly it was just business to them.

The moral to the story is this, I did not educate myself in this field so I wasn't in the know with how detrimental the contract could be. I tried to rap my small mind around a big deal and I made a huge mistake. I had a good heart and good intentions but I did not make a good choice. I could not negotiate what I did not know in the original contract. The lesson along side education is, what you do not know, hire the expert in that field who does before signing your signature.

Never walk into a situation without having an expert on hand to help you argue the point of contracts. Contracts can be written so eloquently with a lot of terms you are not familiar with. Most likely these are legal terms, more reason of why an attorney should handle matters of legal documents.

On the same hand, you may be a good debater and negotiator but you cannot debate or negotiate in every field. Try your best to enlist on your team other great debaters and negotiators. There is power in numbers and more of you is greater than one of you. I learned this lesson the hard way. You don't have to.

## THE POWER OF A CLOSED MOUTH

*Wise men speak because they have something to say, a fool speak because he has to say something.*

*-Plato*

I've had the privilege of studying world religions, many of which have like principles. Most religions endorse the freedom or power of speaking. My particular faith of Christianity heavily deals with ones power to speak. The United States Constitutional right found in the first amendment reinforces the freedom to speak. Every profession known to mankind requires the ability to speak. The deaf and mute community even have ways to speak even without the having the ability to hear or talk. Speaking liberates the mind. Speaking releases the issues of the heart. To speak is to have a voice.

Speaking comes in many forms such as impromptu-on the spot speaking with no specific subject. Manuscript-scripted speeches that are written clearly to be recited. Informative-information driven speaking in its respective fields. The world is driven by those who would dare lift up their voice and society where speaking seems to be the most valuable asset.

Growing up in my particular faith and even now it is so normal to see that everyone has a "word". You would be amazed of how many so-called prophets there are and how many people have a spoken word, word of knowledge, word of prophesy, word of ignorance, word of the day etc. The preacher has a word, the staff has a word, the congregants have a word, the kids have a word. Everybody got a word.

Outside of my faith everyone has something to say. The doctor has a word, the attorney has a word, the shrink has a word, the judge has a word, the talk show host has a word, the rabbi has a word, the imam has a word, and the upasaka has a word. Facebook is full of words; Twitter spearheads the short form word. In a climate of freedom of speech, what has come into question is not the liberty or power to speak, but rather the power in not speaking.

The world is talking and it is of no indication that many people value silence. On one extreme everyone down to the baby has something to say and on the other, those who have something of substance to say don't speak often. You would think that somewhere in the middle of both extremes there is a balance.

Ask a woman how was her day and she's going to give it to you. "Well I woke up this morning and made a cup of coffee. Woke the kids and got them ready for school. I realized that John didn't finished his homework so we got that finished and finally I get them out the door to school. After that I realized that I hadn't been to the gym in a week so I get dressed and went to the gym for an hour. When I left the gym I had to stop by the supermarket to get dinner for tonight. I was in aisle nine and ran into Shirley and can you believe she had back surgery?" By the time she gets done telling you about her day, you will need a drink of something.

It's not just our right to speak, but what I realize is that it's our nature to speak. The thought of not speaking literally will send us as a people into a state of shock. Imagine if one day we woke up and the national news reported that the Supreme Court is debating on whether or not the first amendment is constitutional and is looking to abolish the law. Talking about a civil war on our hands? In the last portion of the code I want to put emphasis on the power of a closed mouth. I must warn you that this will be a strong contrast between the opening of this code.

Silence is the lack of sound, situation; state, or period of time in which no one speak. Silence is the ability to exist in a space with nothing going on around you and in a busy world, it is a hot commodity. To be able to pull away from the noise of work, school, home, the kids, and life in general is of great benefit but not so easy. To seek, learn, and cherish such is like swimming up stream against a robust current.

Just as we have the right legally to speak, we are also within legal rights according to the Fifth Amendment to remain silent. This is found in the Miranda Right section of the Fifth Amendment which protects any person from self-incrimination. Self-incrimination is when a person expose themselves by uttering information at the wrong time.

Not speaking in some cases protects you from you. These are usually the times when we speak prematurely, talking ourselves into situations we cannot talk ourselves out of. Just as we utilize our first amendment, we have the same opportunity to use our fifth amendment.

Every spiritual book talks about quietness or stillness. The scriptures give a unique insight on this matter as it urges to study to be quite. The word study becomes our point of focus. Study is a personal effort to gain knowledge. In a more simple form, it means practice. To study demands time, effort, and attention to detail. To consistently grow in a particular area, studying must be ongoing. One cannot possibly excel on a subject after studying for ten minutes of a twenty-four hour day.

The question we must ask is why does the scripture urge us all to study to be quiet? If quietness was so simple, why must we practice to do so? It leads me to this thought. Because our nature is the complete opposite, it is hard for we as a people to shut out the noise of life or perhaps shut our mouth.

If we are so mentally cluttered with the noise of our lives? How then can we possibly hear with our spiritual ears or see with our spiritual eyes what our creator wants us to know? Moreover, if we are constantly talking, how can we listen to understand what is being said.

While society says speak to be heard, I wonder if silence when necessary has a greater impact. Certainly there is a time and a place for everything. My determination is that winners have a fond appreciation for both the right to speak and the power of not saying anything at all. Silence is a vociferous voice that often speak louder than words.

## CODE SEVEN

## DEFINE YOU

My life principles come from a mixture of great teachers that I've had. All who have taught me great lessons. I was inspired by another former boss and mentor. In the last code I shared the story of my first courtroom experience, not because I was in any trouble with the law but because of a job opportunity. It was from that career experience that I was able to glean insight and truths, some of which I shared in the previous code. Here is another transformative moment.

After transitioning from that firm to another to fill a similar position with higher pay, I encounter a man by the name of Thomas Foley, former Deputy Attorney General turned top defense lawyer in the state of Delaware. Tom was one of three supervisors and was the more hands on attorney who insured that the office had a consistent flow. He did so in a rather peculiar way. He was not the aggressive affirmative kind of guy. Tom was the humble yet confident guy who had a way of dealing with people. He was very generous. I'm sure with his profession he had to be the direct opposite but in the office we got the nice guy.

I had only worked for this firm a few months before I was first summonsed to his office. It was early winter and I left school and headed straight to work. When I arrived at the job, I started prepping my runs to deliver when the secretary told me that when the runs are finished, Mr. Foley would like to see me in his office. I said ok. In my head, I was trying to figure out why. What could be the possible reason why he wants to see me? Did I do something wrong? Did a document mistakenly not get filed in a particular court?

At any rate, I proceeded with my errands for the day and when I got back I went up to his office and knocked on the door. I could hear that he was on the phone and after a pause while he finished up with his phone call he said come. I opened the door and he told me to have a seat. First, he asked me where was I from, I told him I was born and raised right here in Wilmington. He responded that he hasn't met many young men who still use manners in such a way that I did and that I seem to be more southern. I then stated where my roots were and that my family originated in North Carolina. My mother told me that being polite and using my manners would get me favor with people. Her wisdom has proven to be true.

It was at this moment that he began to give me tools for life and how to succeed. What I thought would be a quick meeting turned into more of a lecture. He spoke about how important it was for my image to match my personality. "Thaddeus you are a great young man with a great personality, but if first impression is all some will get from you, then they will never know how great of a guy you are" he said. He went on to say that in the world in which we live, I must dress and carry myself in a way that successful people will want to know whom I was and what I do for a living.

The truth is, in those days I was attracted to the lifestyle of corporate businessmen. I wanted to have that kind of lifestyle. To be able to have the nice houses, cars, and even one day send my children to college paid for by dad. The problem was, I dressed and carried myself as if I was a product of the environment that I was raised in. I wanted to fit in the hood and I failed miserably at trying to dress and carry my self like the guys I saw in the street. I wore the pants off of my behind not knowing the origin, grew my hair long so that I could have it braided, twisted, or whatever was the fad then. And it simply wasn't who I God intended for me to be.

At the very moment while sitting in Tom's office I had my hair blown out in a massive Afro that looked like I stuck my hand in a socket. It appeared as if I was being electrocuted. He gave me pointers about a variety of things such as making good eye contact when shaking hands and even how to choose what to wear based on the occasion. The more he talked, the more I would soak up. His way of presenting his point of view was in such a was, it was easy to receive without taking offense to it. It wasn't that I didn't know better or wanted to do better, I just needed that good talking to that everyone could use every now and again.

Mr. Foley concluded our meeting by stating that he wanted to take the staff out to lunch for Christmas and he wanted me to attend. The stipulations were that I had to get permission from my parents, dress appropriate, and to do something with my hair. None of which would be a problem. In curiosity I asked, what do you suggest I do with my hair? He responded, "Son if you want to be the successful man I know one day you'll be, cut it off". For some that may sound ridiculous, as there are many successful people in a verity of cultures and creeds with wild hairstyles. For me, a young man who was in a bit of an identity crisis, that's all I needed to hear. I went home that day, went to the barbershop and had it all chopped off. It was a lot of hair and I had an attachment to my hair but I believed in the counsel I was given. I saw proven results from the counselor himself.

This was no ordinary restaurant that we were going to. Tom ensured that I knew just where we were going and the caliber of place it was. He told me that we would be having lunch at the Brandywine Country Club. I never heard of this place or knew what a country club was but it sound grand. So I asked, what is the Brandywine Country Club exactly, he told me that it was an award winning gulf course that you had to be a member of. Of course I wanted to know how do you become a member and he said that "hard work and about six thousand dollars would get me a membership." I'm thinking six thousand dollars for what? But ok.

The day came that we were to have lunch and that morning all the staff showed up at the office. It was six of us total that left from the office and three others that met us there. Tom said to me that he wanted me to ride with him in the front while the secretary and another attorney rode the back seat. So we get into his new black Lexus sedan to head for the restaurant. He looks over on the passenger side where I was sitting and says before we go, I have to make at stop at my house to pick up something. I said ok, unsure of why he decided to tell me that and not to mention there are others in the car. Why not address the entire car?

About five minutes later we arrived at his house, as it was stationed right on the outskirts of Wilmington in the 19806 area code. The 19806 is known to be an area where influential people live and who obviously were well off financially however, this was not what I expected. Although I'm sure the house was pretty expensive, this was more of a modest brick townhouse surrounded by houses you would consider mansions. With further thought it matched his personality, wealthy but not over the top. He got out of the car went into the house for a few seconds and came back out.

When he got back into the car he looked at me once again and asked, are you ready? I said yes. He rebutted, "Thaddeus you're gonna like this. Don't be nervous." As we were driving to the club, he leaned over discretely and asked do you know your table setting? I hadn't taken etiquette classes so the question sounded foreign and I said no. He said its simple, just start on the outside and work your way in. After a while, it really doesn't matter anyway he said, you'll do just fine. He had music playing softly so that our conversation was intimate and the ladies in the back could not here. It was more like man talk.

Finally we get to the country club after riding for roughly ten minutes and from the parking lot it seemed like a normal place. There was a building situated on a well-manicured lawn. We pull up to the door and get out as Tom hands the key to the gentlemen to park the car. We walk in and what didn't seem too spectacular from the outside instantly wowed me on the inside. We were met with dim lighting, elegant décor and impeccable service. That was enough for me and I was sold. Tom was greeted at the door personally and it was obvious that he had a working relationship with everyone there.

When we arrived at the table that was reserved for our group, we were seated. The table was elegantly arrayed with china that didn't resemble those at your local Olive Garden or Red Lobster. The table was perfectly station under a beautifully lit crystal chandelier with that same lighting bouncing off of the water and wine glasses. What sealed the deal for me was when I picked up the menu only to discover that nothing was cheap. Tom had already informed me not to be concerned with prices because he was picking up the bill for everyone. After seeing that menu I was glad. I ordered a crab cake with coke and waited as everyone else placed his or her order.

After everyone ordered what they were having, Tom thanked every one for coming. Holidays are special he said and I wanted to reward everyone for their hard work. He then reached into his suit jacket and handed everyone an envelope. Initially I received it and placed it in my suit jacket. Open it he said to the table, so I reached in my jacket and pulled the envelope back out. When I opened up the envelope I was shocked at the number I saw. The check tripled my weekly salary. I didn't want to seem overly excited so I smiled and said thank you. The remainder of our lunch was full of talk of current affairs, office bloopers, politics, and of course the celebration surrounding the holiday season.

What I took from the experience was that I was a combination of a history, present experiences and future ambitions. I do not believe Mr. Foley intent was to force his perception of me on me. I believe that he wanted me to learn valuable principles at an early age and expose me to another of level of life to challenge my view of myself. When I added these components, it became easy for to start defining who I really am and not who I thought I was or who others thought I should be. Past, present, and future helped me to bring definition to myself.

## YOU HAVE YOUR DEFINITION

If you asked yourself today, what is my definition, would you be able to answer the question in a single statement? If so, how accurate would that statement be? A part of winning is ones ability to precisely bring definition to their life. This means that the winner knows their mission, intent, style, flavor, likes, and dislikes.

You are a collision of your inner most being and outer expression. Who you are on the inside starts to manifest on your person, so how you are feeling at the moment will show. The importance of you being your best on the inside is key. You want to exude all of the good things that are in your heart and to do so you have to keep you in a good place.

Who you are is extremely important to the world and until you can define who you are, you become vulnerable to the definitions of others. I will show you in a moment why you must be motivated to do so. The winner must know without a doubt their true definition and if you do not know the definition of you, you cannot expect others to. You have to know you better than anyone else and it is at that point that you can innately stand and share with others what makes you uniquely you.

What you cannot define has no value. People invest time, energy, and money where they see value. So then your worth is in your definition. What defines you tells a lot about your purpose and your net worth. Your definition will set boundaries not just for others but also for yourself. These boundaries insure that your assets are protected because your value is at an all time high.

What is your mission? By now you should know what your purpose is as I have shared the fundamentals of purpose in my previous codes. Your mission is the action behind your purpose that makes you wake up in the morning and spend every waking moment fulfilling that purpose. Your mission is your daily journey to be everything God created you to be in the earth. With that understanding you take advantage of every option to accomplish the mission.

Winners with a mission don't intentionally make frequent pit stops. Pit stops are those small stops on the road to destiny that may be necessary but not a priority. These individuals plan before hand to avoid stopping along the way because it slows progress. Rather than jumping on the road only to have to stop for laboratory purposes or refueling at an odd time, these individuals gather all things needed for the journey, use the restroom and fuel the car.

Years ago, I remember my family taking frequent trips to a small town called Harrellsville, North Carolina where my mother's family originated prior to migrating to Delaware. Harrellsville is a far stretch from the metropolitan city in which I grew up. In fact, this place is as country as it gets in my view. There isn't much there except farmland, the same farmland that my mother and her seven siblings grew up on. There are no streetlights, no corner stores, no shopping malls, not much of anything. There is one gas station in the entire town.

These were trips that we loved to take mainly because that's where my grandmother lived. It was those times when we'd drive for six hours through several states to see grandma and others that we didn't see often, as we like. My siblings and I enjoyed the various sights as we traveled through different cultural locations of the east coast. We'd go from city to rural to countryside and it was amazing to see how different life was just hours apart. It was indeed an adventure.

What I cannot forget was the preparation that my mother put into the trip. My father was responsible for all the driving so his prep time was to sleep. The day before we were to leave my mother would spend the day helping us pack. She would make sure that we were dressed appropriately for the weather and that we had the essentials. Whatever we didn't have according to her liking we would have to go buy. This day would consist of mom going to the supermarket to buy food. She didn't believe in spending money on the way for food but determined that it was more time and cost efficient to bring our own. This would alleviate the need to stop for meals. Mom cooked every meal from scratch and individualized them.

We usually left our house early - around six in the morning so mom made sure that we were ready to go. We would get up in the morning already bathed from the night before. We would get dressed, have breakfast, pray, and then on to the mission. My dad made sure that the car was filled with gas so that we would have no reason to get it before the trip was scheduled to began. By start time we were well prepared and all we had to do was get in the car and go leaving little or no time to stop unless we absolutely had to.

That's the idea of the winner's mission. After determining what the destination or goal is you must figure out how to get there without small distractions that will slow you down. The preparation you put into your mission defines how important your mission is and how determined you are to complete it. Prolonging your mission will gradually cause you to become anxious, tedious and ultimately frustrate your intent of why you're on the mission.

So you have a mission, but what is your intent? Not intent as in purpose. In what way do you intend to win on all levels? When defining who you are, knowing how your going to fulfill your mission is key. For example, one of the painstaking moments for the Obama Administration to capture Osama Bin Laden was knowing the best way to capture the guy who did the unthinkable on our soil. The mission was clear, we had to find him to bring him to justice, how was the question.

With the assistance of his national security team and advisors, the President was able to agree with a drafted plan on how the mission was to be carried out. The mission was a defining point in his first term and for his presidency. Firstly, it said whether or not he was capable of being commander and chief of the strongest military in the world. Secondly, it defined whether or not he should be reelected for a second term.

Choosing a route is important because it will determine when you get there and where you will end up once your there. On a map you can have one destination and two to three different routes to get there. I had some business to tend to in New York City for the day not long ago. Because I had to be on one end of the city for the first half and on the other side of the city for the second half, I concluded that it would be easier for me to drive as appose to catching the bus or train as I normally would. I get in the car that morning and programed the address to the hotel that I was scheduled to be into maps on my iPhone. When I plugged in the address it gave me a few routes to take from Delaware to New York City. Among the routes that I chose were those that would have allowed me to avoid a few tolls and another that would have allowed me to avoid almost every toll. Although I would have saved money by avoiding the tolls with the alternative choices, it would have taken longer to get there. Of course, I ended up taking the shorter route that cost me more.

When defining your mission, you will not always have the luxury of saving on the front end. Sometimes you have to suck it up a pay the price of destiny. Your mission in life will cost you because your destiny holds unlimited and untapped value. Those who take the cheap route out will take much longer to get there and it will shed light on the person's definition. It will show how cheap he or she is when it comes to their future.

No one has the right to define you. People will try to define so that you can fit into their idea of who you are in their world. Usually these people will employ manipulation tactics to get you to conform to their idea. You will hear some people overly suggest things to you that just don't fit your character. For example, the conversation with this individual would go as such…*Sarah, I really see you in news broadcasting. You have the perfect face and voice for that career field. Why don't you look into going to school for that? Maybe when you graduate you can help me launch my media company.*

Here is the problem, Sarah is shy and doesn't like the attention on her. Sarah has no desire of having a career in broadcasting. In fact Sarah wants to be veterinarian because she has always been a lover of animals. She always dreamed of growing up to be one who cared for animals and as a result, Sarah perused her education in that field.

Notice that the person admonishing her to get into broadcasting has an agenda. The individual starts by telling Sarah what they see about Sarah. Then he or she tells Sarah all good reasons of why she should get into that field. Lastly, the true motive of why this person wants Sarah to be a news broadcaster is revealed and it's to ultimately to have Sarah do something for them, even if it has nothing to do with Sarah's life purpose.

People who attempt to define you or try to force fit you in their idea are most likely self-centered and manipulative. The correct term is called narcissism. Narcissism is the fascination with ones self and ideas that seek gratification based on vain admirations. These individuals care about nothing but there agenda. If it is of no benefit to them in some way then it is of no value to them. Narcissistic people will only invest in what is of value to them as it relates to people. If you refuse to fit in their idea then you are considered one who is opposing them.

A person who is a narcissist usually has a hard time empathizing with others. They can never imagine putting themselves in other people shoes to see from that point of view. For instance, a person who is consumed with themselves will not seek to understand why a homeless person is without what would be considered the basics of life. They will pass judgment as to why they are without. Because a narcissist is not empathetic, being sympathetic will most likely be non-existent.

Narcissism does not allow someone to have sympathy for others' misfortunes. A person can be at their lowest point in life and perhaps only needing some encouragement. One who is full of their self will ignore the unfortunate's need and play on their emotions to somehow turn the situation to satisfy what they want. This kind of person is emotionless to those who are experiencing hardships. This will often cause a narcissist to use people to their advantage at the expense of the person they are using. Most likely the person being used will pick up the tab thinking they are doing some good deed.

The self-absorbed person will choose the "false humility" facade to further an agenda to emotionally control another person. This is another manipulation tactic that's used to sway people into the unseen advantage to be taken advantage of. A simple example, you run into Brian at the mall and wanted to compliment Brian on his success at the job. Not knowing that Brian is a narcissist you continue to tell him how great of a guy he is and how he deserved the awards he received for the outstanding work he's been doing. You proceed to tell Brian that he's the best worker that the team has. Brian says thank you but he does not really value your opinion. He will appear to be humbly gracious for your praise while seeking a way to have you come under his tutelage with an agenda that wouldn't be in your best interest. Because Brian is self-centered, he will find some way to use you. He will perhaps have you work on a project with himself with the notion that if it goes wrong, he will place all the blame on you. He will use his track record as his point of reference to keep him in the clear and you essentially become his pawn and scapegoat.

I researched a man by the name of Erik Erikson, a German born American developmental psychologist. Although he lacked a Bachelor's degree, his brilliance led him to serve as professor at elite colleges such as Yale and Harvard. His writings on issues of human development are noteworthy and from which the phrase "identity crisis" was coined. As I explored his research findings as it relates to identity crisis, I was intrigued.

Erikson's medical determination on identity crisis suggest a strong identity evolves not only from a thorough scrutiny of your life's purpose, but also resolving childhood developmental challenges from your past. Having a solid identity in your childhood rests on your having a strong sense of trust in infancy stages, independence in toddlerhood, ability to play as a preschooler and a strong work ethic in elementary stages. Erikson hailed that the issues of life may re-emerge in adulthood especially those of dysfunction. You may confront problems in your connection to work in your young adult years if you feel as if your job is a dead end. On the same hand, you may confront issues in your later life from your early years. For example, those who are coping with childhood trauma such as rejection could face psychosocial issues later on in adulthood. I dealt with this particular instance more deeply in code two.

An identity crisis can surface at any point in your life when your challenged to face your sense of self. When this confrontation takes place, you seem to have no idea who and what you are, where you belong in life, and where you want to go. This will cause you to retract from the real world not getting in the game of life. Such a crisis has great potential to cause some to turn to drugs, violence, promiscuity, pornography and so on as a way if coping with identity crisis. Erikson determined that someone having an identity crisis is more prone to having a negative identity rather than none at all.

Another concept of identity crisis is ones uncertainty of their role in society. Often times those who suffer from this syndrome are unsure where they fit in a huge world of all kinds of people. It is my philosophy that all though your designed to stand out, there is a perfect fit for your peculiarity in ways that are beneficial to society. One who can positively identify their self is a powerful force internally and externally.

People who are experiencing an identity crisis often have a lapse in memory of the past. Those who struggle with finding ones self do not remember much of their childhood or events dating back a decade or more. History is full of hidden truths and without knowing those truths due to the lapses in memory, it's hard to understand who you are. I've stated before that you cannot understand you without knowing where you come from.

You don't have to die having never lived due to this crisis. You can start living right now by discovering your true self. Search out your family tree, your childhood, you inner most desire, and where you would like to end up in life. Uncover suppressed issues and win starting now.

# CODE EIGHT

# BRAND

There is a story of two rival companies and how their brand got them to the peak of the soda industry, one being Pepsi-Cola and the other Coca-Cola. The rivalry has been long hailed as the "cola wars" and for over a century they would share dominance in the beverage market with a marketing strategy called brand and rebranding.

Caleb Bradman, a pharmacist who wanted to create a fountain drink, founded Pepsi in 1893 in New Bern, North Carolina. Bradman created his version of cola inside his drug store where he sold it until business progressed causing him to move his bottling to a larger warehouse in 1903. That year, through increased production, he sold 7,698 gallons. The year after by just changing the bottle size Bradman was able to increase sells to 19,848 gallons.

Like most companies today, Caleb Bradman needed a face to get his product exposure to a broader audience. He would not get the company's first break until 1909 when auto racer Barney Oldfield, the first man to drive a car at sixty miles per hour, endorsed Pepsi-Cola. Oldfield described the drink as "a bully drink, invigorating, and a bracer before a race". Soon after while trying find its identity, Pepsi would through two logo designs in just three years.

Pepsi however would fall victim to the great depression by 1931 forcing Bradman to enter the company into bankruptcy. After everything was sold, what was left of the brand was sold to a guy named Roy Megargel. After Roy discovered he didn't have what it took to build the company into a success, he then sold it to Charles Guth. Guth was president of Loft, Inc. Loft was a candy manufacturer that had a chain of store that so happened to sell Coca-Cola. He saw an opportunity to replace Coca-Cola in his stores by having Loft's chemist reformulate the existing Pepsi syrup.

Later on when the great depression was nearing its end, Pepsi received notoriety after the introduction of their twelve-ounce bottle. This was six more ounces than the previous bottle upgrade received in 1904. As Pepsi embarked on a new marketing campaign to promote its new size, they launched a radio campaign with the jingle "Pepsi Cola hits the spot; twelve full ounces that's a lot. Twice as much for a nickel too, Pepsi Cola is the drink for you". The company arrayed the song so that it would loop but never end. I actually heard two different original versions of the jingle when on YouTube and thought it was clever and catchy, especially for that time. It's indeed a classic.

Pepsi would then launch its competitive campaign, another marketing strategy against Coke; it's all-time rival. They challenged the consumer to price watch as Pepsi offered almost double the amount of soda than Coke's six and a half ounce bottle for the same price. This was a tactic that literally undercut its competitor simply because more for the buck has always been the consumers' agenda. With this strategy, Pepsi for the first time was able to succeed and double its profits from 1936-1938.

Charles Guth would eventually enter into a legal battle with Loft Incorporated, a Delaware corporation, over the rights to Pepsi-Cola. The case went all the way to the Delaware Supreme Court with the argument that Guth was in breach of fiduciary loyalty to the company he headed by not offering the opportunity to Loft first. Although Guth bought the brand, he used Loft's facilities and chemist to remix the syrup that makes the soda what it is. The Chief Justice of the Court concluded that Charles Guth violated basic principles of conflict of interest and as a result he lost his case.

Walter Mack gained control of Pepsi as the new president and saw that the previous marketing strategy was not in favor of African Americans and that it in fact ignored the minority based audiences. To appeal to the African American consumer, he hired an all black sales team with Edward Boyd, an executive who specialized in marketing to African Americans who had been disenfranchised to lead the team of twelve. By targeting the black audience alone saw a rise in the market share of the company. The think tank came up with its latest marketing strategy that portrayed blacks as it really was in those days. What they portrayed was the true image of our home life consisting of an American family who happened to be of the black race. Pepsi launched new advertising showing a black mother holding a six-pack over her son as he anticipated cracking open a bottle. This proved to be what the company needed and it was a great success.

Pepsi would not get that kind of success over its leading competitor Coke again until 1975 when it launched its Pepsi Challenge. Pepsi Challenge was a marketing campaign were the company set up blind taste testing between Pepsi-Cola and competitor Coca-Cola. The blind taste test revealed most soft beverage consumers preferred the Pepsi brand over Coke's and the company would use this to their advantage by televising it nationally through commercials showing the results.

Since that time Pepsi would go through a series of brand and marketing strategies, overhauling their logo and slogans to remain in an ever progressive and competitive market. By creating a brand that demanded consumer's attention and rebranding what has already been established, they were able to reach success points. Coca-Cola however branded their product much differently.

Coca-Cola was created by John Pemberton, a Columbus, Georgia based pharmacist who was addicted to morphine. John Pemberton wanted to find a substitute for the drug and began mixing in his Georgia drug store until he came up with the original Coca-Cola recipe found in his signature drink called the Coca Wine. From this derived the infamous suggestion that Coca-Cola was once laced with cocaine, which is actually the truth. The Coca Wine that Pemberton created was a mixture of the syrup used in Coca-Cola along with cocaine and alcohol.

The popular Coca Wine would eventually dissolve around 1886 after the state of Georgia introduced prohibition and banned the use of alcohol forcing Pemberton to reformulate his syrup with out the use of alcohol. Due to the fear of drug addiction, the United States prohibited the use of cocaine and the removal from the wine as well as the Coca strand from the actual soda. After the United States put a ban on alcohol, the Coca Wine altogether became illegal.

This forced John Pemberton to focus on his Coca-Cola fountain drink and by 1888 he entered into partnership with four Atlanta based businessman. Together they would put out three different versions of the soda, a move that would prove to be unsuccessful and eventually sending the brand through a mixture of business deals and battles over rights to the name. After the death of John Pemberton the deal was clarified and said to have been one between Charley his son and Asa Candler who bought the majority stake in the company with John acting as a co-signer on the deal.

With Asa Candler having majority stake, he incorporated what is now known as the Coca-Cola Company. The company again went through many changes with Candler's full control due to a deal to give the bottling process to two businessmen who moved it from Georgia to Tennessee. The two businessmen then formed the Coca-Cola Bottling Company, which proved to be another failed decision for the company causing legal problems to ensue. My study doesn't give me how exactly the matter was settled but I'm sure that there was some sort of agreement.

It wouldn't be until 1935 that Coca-Cola would officially become the poster board for soft drinks rising to the top of the market. Coca-Cola has since remained Americas most preferred soda only rendering the title on occasion to Pepsi. It would even receive the endorsement from an Atlanta base rabbi who rendered the drink kosher after a series of changes in the syrup's ingredients.

I've watched a few of Coca-Cola's early TV commercials from the 50's and noticed that the target audience even for this brand didn't just Ignore minorities but it appeared to ignore men as well. The first TV commercials that Coke produced seemed to target the Caucasian stay at home mom that shopped for her family. Although the commercials would say the drink was for "smart shoppers" and show snippets of men, in those days men did not do much shopping at all. It then made since as to why the Pepsi brand expanded their reach and succeeded in doing so.

Coca-Cola however had a rather unique way of marketing their brand and to the contrary of their competitor, they didn't undergo as many changes. By the time that Coca-Cola would firmly claim their stake as number one, other soda brands would campaign on a verity of slogans. Coke's position was to remain on the offense and market their soda as "the real thing". The slogan was quite brilliant and allowed the company to remain focus for the most part on the product rather than its competitors. Almost as if to say all other brands that came after our inception with their variation of the cola was a counterfeit. This is why branding is so important.

Branding is the ongoing process of making a mark that cannot easily be erased. From a business view, "brand" is a conglomerate of associations directly connected to a person's view of a company, product and it's services. The unfortunate thing about this is that the words "brand" And "branding" have been loosely used in modern culture. I took the initiative to type in Amazon books search engine the word "brand" and over 1.3 million books have been written on this subject, All having 1.3 million perspectives on this topic.

Since we've already examined the Coca-Cola's brand idea, let's look further. Coke is revered as the king of soda but it's the might of the brand that makes it a powerful force. A Coke executive once hailed that "If Coca-Cola were to lose all of it production-related assets in a disaster, the company would survive. By contrast, if all consumers were to have a sudden lapse of memory and forget everything related to Coca-Cola, the company would go out of business".

When a person thinks of Coke, immediately you think of the obvious. You think of things that are most commonly associated with the drink such as, "It's the real thing", that it's an all American favorite turned global best seller, it's the original cola, the classic glass bottle or the red can. Or perhaps the stigma behind the drink and its former content of cocaine is what you would associate with the brand. Whether or not your association to the product is good or bad or if you even drank the soda, you cannot ignore the presence of Coke. That's because of its dominating force.

## MARKET YOUR PERSONA

I used the rivalry of the two beverage brands with intent to show you how effective branding can be. Brands aren't limited to the food industry or any other industry and if the model work for corporations than it can work for people. Elton John is a brand name. Steve Harvey is a brand name. Jay Z is a brand name. Jimmy Fallon is a brand name. These are individuals who have branded themselves in such a way that even if you are not fans, you still know who they are and what's associated with them.

Personal branding is selling individuals or corporations your personality. It behooves the winner to think hard about how to carry ones self especially in the public eye. You should have a clear identifiable personality so that your audience feels connected to who you are and what you have to offer. This doesn't take much effort to do because you're simply being you at its best. The worst thing you can do is attempt to immolate someone else, as you will be marketing his or her personality instead of yours. Those who know both you and the person you are immolating will know that you not being original.

You are the face of your "big Idea" and sometimes the only association others will have with your idea is your personality. Your personality can be methodical, friendly, and humorous at the same time. All traits that is essential to getting your brand in the arena it needs to be.

Your personality is what you're remembered by after the conversation is finished and you will past that encounter of the day. Combine your personal style with your tone of voice (which is the verbiage you use along with social skills and you will be off to a great start.

## YOUR PERSONAL STYLE

One of the most important elements for the winner to define ones' self is establishing their brand. Branding will help you stand out from your peers, add value to your definition, and help you engage with your followers. Your followers will be more prone to recognize you and your associations by knowing your personal brand. Your personal brand in many ways is synonymous with your personality. The way you display your personality through style, communication and tone are all key ways to begin your branding process.

Your personal brand should speak volumes of who you are even if you do not have a website, blog, or business card. Let's put a focus on individual style and to do so we must differentiate style from fashion. You see, fashion or trends come and go but style is classic and never fluctuate. It was in times past that a person was defined as successful by the way they dressed. For example, a man was viewed as successful businessman if he was well dressed in a tailored suit. That's certainly not the case anymore.

In America today there are two types of billionaires. There are the billionaires of Wall Street and there are the billionaires of the tech industry in Silicon Valley. The interesting contrast between the two is that the Wall Street billionaire you will most likely see if not in a tailor made suit, at least in the likes of Brioni or Hickey Freeman. Where as the Silicon Valley billionaire would most likely prefer the ripped jeans, t-shirt, and sneakers. Both are obviously very successful and very rich but have two different style preferences.

When branding yourself the style you choose is important because remember you are your definition and your style will invite others to inquire what that definition is. In a more simplistic way, you are "the gift" but your gift-wrapping draws others to the gift. You can buy the most expensive gift but if the gift is poorly wrapped, it could sit for days or even weeks before anyone is interested enough to open it. Your personal style is your packaging.

My personal style is one that is more eclectic, one style preference being a well tailored suit. When the occasion calls for me to wear one, I wear it well and that's intentional. In terms of what particular style of suit I prefer would lean more towards the modern British style. There is a more simplistic clean look when you think of British tailoring. I believe a man should dress in such a way that he looks nice but you cant quite figure out what it is. The secret is in the tailoring. It's the fit. A man should not resort to loudness of the colors or the mixing of stripes and polka dots to stand out although it can be done tastefully. I'm not at all against Italian tailoring. The Italians have mastered and dominated their brand of suit for decades. I do own one or two myself.

When you think of British tailoring you commonly associate it with English royalty such as Prince Charles. Prince Charles is one who knows something about personal branding as it relates to ones style in suits. Take a moment to Google him and click on images and what you will see is a man who's always dressed in a suit. The particular style of suit he is dressed in will normally if not always be a British bespoke double-breasted suit. You would think that it's his uniform and for him, it is. Prince Charles' choice to suit up and his chosen style of suit is what he uses to brand himself.

Another one of my personal styles is the American boy look, which leans towards Abercrombie & Fitz, Hollister, or even American Eagle. My opinion is that this particular look is one that epitomizes American everyday culture. The look within itself can make the CEO look like the average approachable guy or girl who would not otherwise seem down to earth. Because I'm more of the coffee house, bookstore kind of guy, not only does it fit me but also it helps me interact with different kinds of people.

The "American boy" or "American Girl" style is one that is cross racial and cross cultural. Here in the

U.S. it has become a favorite among those who live here regardless of race or social background. Whites, Blacks, Koreans, Chinese, Indians and all other races will be found wearing this particular style. This would be the reason why there is an upspring and expansion of such clothing brands. By all accounts, these stores are in demand as places to shop.

In an interesting contrast, I was watching a documentary on Savile Row's history. At the start of the show the director took the viewer from tailoring house to tailoring house such Anderson & Shepard, Gieves & Hawkes, Huntsman, and the more modern Cad & The Dandy. Each of these representatives shared their particular specialty in bespoke suits, their account of history of the row, and their anxiety of what the row is becoming. As I continued to watch, the various persons being interview shared how newcomers on the row that did not specialize in bespoke tailoring would dilute the rich heritage of Savile Row.

They continued to share what they believed to be a direct threat in light of Abercrombie & Fitz, a blue jean company buying a former bank building on the row. A&B planted a store and was preparing for the grand opening. The Location of the building is so uniquely position that it would be near impossible to miss. The challenge that the tailors were having physiologically was that although there was still a great need for bespoke tailoring, it was no longer the standard even in a place like London. London was evolving and struggling to meet the need of modern culture and old English way of living. It was experiencing sort of a culture shock.

Later in the documentary, the two worlds would meet and although the tailors didn't like what was taking place, they had to face the music. I continued to watch and while one of the tailors were interviewing, in walks the head of Abercrombie Mike Jeffries, the sixty odd sum year old CEO. Jeffries was dressed rather youthfully just as his advertisements and wanted to meet his fellow designers as he called it. That's not how the tailors viewed each other. I'm sure Jefferies knew that his business wasn't welcomed on the row but it didn't stop him from being the good guy and introducing himself. In an odd twist of event, Jeffries ended up getting a bespoke suit made. While the tailors couldn't fathom wearing jeans, the king of blue jeans understood that there was a need for both.

Last, there is my most comfortable and favorite style of dressing. I always try to find an even balance in all aspects of my life and as it relates to dressing my balance is a mixture between conservative and casual. The reason being is that it's always safe. A person's day can began one way and through a change of unexpected events, the day could end up a totally different way. My philosophy with style and dressing is to remain neutral because regardless of what my day will entail, for the most part I'll be prepared.

Let me reiterate, a vital part of communicating your brand and its idea is how you package yourself. Ninety percent of the people that will listen to what you have to say will first judge your package. If your outer package in this case style, class and charisma which equals you presentation is not attractive, then you lose a big chunk of your or audience or potential audience. You cannot win without an audience.

## REBRAND YOUR IMAGE

To understand what your image should look like is to know that you were made in "HIS" image. God is a spirit so certainly I'm not speaking of image is in physicality but rather the image of God contains characteristics and attributes that we possess. So to look like God is strictly in principle and when God sees you, what he's looking for his reflection. You essentially mirror all of the great things about God such as his strength, power, love, forgiveness, grace and so on.

In the beginning of time as we know it when God created the vegetation and animals, He created them after their own kind. To the contrary, when He created Adam and Eve, He created them after His image and likeness or the "God kind". After Adams disobedience to God, the image of man was defiled and no longer mirrored God in its totality. This was the perfect job for Christ who is the expressed image of God in both heaven and earth. Christ came to restore our tarnished image the God seeks while looking at us by standing in the middle presenting us faultless.

For the Christian, our goal is to look more and more like God by projecting his characteristics. So then if we pose the question, who is God? All of us would be able to give our definition of God based on our intellectual ability. That would either be by what we've read about God, what we were told about God or what we've experienced with God. All of which are valid definitions according you the individual. But, God is more than the human mind can comprehend. One thing I think all people of all faiths can agree upon is this. God is love.

Love is in fact an attribute of God and I want to take a moment to talk about how to walk in love as you are now rebranding your image. The love for God, family, passion, and equality as important, the love for people will help you succeed. You will not be able to win on any level with out love and for this reason anything you do must be centered around it. For love is the ultimate power for anyone to hold.

Love will help you forgive those who have wronged you. The reason being is that love is not self-righteous. You have not always as a human being done the right thing towards others. You have in times past did or said something offensive towards someone else. It's a human error that you're not exempt from and knowing that should cause to forgive others who are within the same human error. Love doesn't remember faults but it makes you remember that you can at anytime be at fault. A common example could be something so simple as a parking spot. Say you drive into your local Wal-Mart attempting to park and just as you approach the ideal parking spot right in front of the door, another car hurry's to pull in right before you. Maybe they did see you with your turn signal and chose to purposely take your spot. Love helps you forgive that person by causing you to remember the time you were that other car.

*...And be not conformed to this world: but be ye transformed by the renewing of your mind, that ye may prove what is that good, and acceptable, and perfect, will of God.*

*Romans 12:2*

Only you have the power to change how others view you based on past successes and failures. Believe it or not, you're judged on the two but there is a way to carefully recreate and display a new you. One of the ways is to transform. I dealt with this in code two in " the process of becoming" and I want to pick it up from this view briefly. Transformation is a dramatic change in form or appearance. Transformation is inevitable and whether or not you transform for the better or for worse is solely your decision.

Transformation begins with your thinking. Who you think you are, you will become. What you think you can achieve, with persistence in the face of resistance you will achieve. Paul the Apostle challenged the mental state of the reader in this fashion. He uses the word "world" to magnify the unseen word in the passage "kingdom". "World" meaning a democratic like system or thinking and "kingdom" meaning a royal system or thinking. A democracy is a system where by representatives are elected. Elect means to be chosen by vote. The root word for conformed is the word "con" meaning to deceive. So then here is my view of what Paul wanted us to see as it relates to winning by rebranding your image.

Do not deceive yourself into thinking that winning is done by a vote. You don't have to be elected to win. No one determines when you start winning again. Winners think and operate from a royal perspective, a place of privilege. Your heavenly father is God and you are His child. You've been privileged to win as long as you think so. The thing about thinking so is doing it when it is less convenient or it doesn't seem as though you are. It's not until then you can have proof of Gods will for your life. The proof is in the thinking. To rebrand yourself daily into Gods image, you must think like God.

## TRANSFORMATION REQUIRES TRANSISTION

I often say people will come back to the place where they left you expecting you to still be there. For the person who has accepted defeat and feel like that cannot go on, they most likely will. The winner on the other hand will not still be in that place because he or she would have transformed into a wiser, stronger and greater person that reflect God in a more visible way.

One of the hardest things to come to grips with concerning transformation is that you have to let go of people who left you. Transformation allows you to evolve and grow and sometimes you just out grow people. Never hold on to people that want to make an exit out of your life. If they were meant to be there they would be, who knows? Maybe they are but for there own reasons just don't want to, It's okay. You will not die just because they no longer have a place in your space. You have to keep it moving.

We live in a world where everything is moving at such a fast pace. One thing is for sure, life is consistently moving and it will move with or without you. One component of transformation is moving on and moving up. You have to move on from where you are in your life; you cannot stay in the same place. Since you have to move, why not in an upward position? To move on yet remain on the same level isn't much progress. The idea is to aim high and jump until you reach your goal.

Here is the concept. Horizontal movement allows you to move across the level your on. For example, let's say you work for a company and decide that you wanted to move around by applying for other positions. Like most fortune five hundred companies today, you'd apply and if offered the position you would actually still be on the same tier with the same pay grade just in a different spot. The psychology of it is to make you think that you were promoted when in all reality you were replanted in the same place. Promotion is the act of moving higher and to a more important position. Promotions will usually entail more responsibility, which requires a compensation to match.

Vertical movement is rather different and using the same example, vertical movement will allow you to not just move in the same tier or pay grade, it will put you in the position to climb the latter of success. Vertical mobility changes your position in the social, pay, and leadership hierarchy so not only do you have a new position but also you have a new level.

Transition is designed to change your condition and location. It changes everything around you. Not all those that are connected to you will be able to handle the new you. Have you ever heard someone say "now that they have that promotion, they think that their all that"? Implying the one who was promoted on the job isn't acting like their normal self. Well, the reason being is when promotion hits your life you automatically in nature rise to the occasion. You began transitioning into that space. In this case typically the person who made the statement cannot handle the fact that the one who was promoted is now in a position of authority over them.

There is power in moving and you moving keep you in the flow of life. The ability to be in transit from one place to another is one of the most freeing experiences. Nothing happens when your stationed for too long but when your train leaves the station, no matter how long the journey may take you are ok because you're on board and on your way. So it is with your brand. Your brand has to be one that is not only moving from one stage to another, but it must be so big that it moves others. Your brand must have the power to move mountains in someone's life. You transforming will move others to follow you until they get all that you can offer and launch out to go after their dream.

## NEVER LET ANYONE TAKE AWAY YOUR HUMAITY

You are a spiritual being having a human experience. What that means is you will forever make mistakes, some big and others small. As long as you exist as a natural being, you will have natural things that occur like divorce, sickness, loss of love ones, financial challenges etc. No matter how overly you spiritualize things, life still happens. Life happens to the best of them and it happens to the worst off of them.

When rebranding yourself, this time leave room for you to mess up. Whatever ever you do, don't allow others to make you feel unworthy or incompetent just because you made a mess of a situation. Don't let others opinions of you dictate your future all because of their attempt to make you supernatural. The interesting thing about people who are imperfect is that they tend to gain a self-righteous and condescending attitude towards your imperfections. When this happens, you have messed up people that judge other messed up people as if they aren't messed up their self.

The rebranded you should not be one that appears to have at all together. The new you should occasionally display imperfections of character, appearance, and judgment. This will keep you connected with others for the sake of relating to them and it will keep you humble. But if you allow others to rob you of this, you stand pay a steep price.

## NEVER CHASE RUMORS

A good portion of your brand is your reputation. What those who seek to remove you from your humanity will do is take bad press about you that may or may not be true and share it with your audience. These individuals are more likely those who are on a level beneath yours and because it's harder to climb the latter, they would rather nock it over to bring you down to their level. For some it's their hobby and for others it's their occupation. Those who do it, as their profession understands the importance of good and bad publicity. Both can be used in a positive way or to your benefit. These individuals are usually learned in this field and have a degree in broadcasting or journalism. All others who do not have credentials are renegades and should not be taken serious.

There is a reason why a press core has its place. Have you ever noticed that when you've attended a major event that there were a group of individuals wearing badges representing their respective companies holding recorders, cameras and microphones? That's what a press core does, report information. Most organizations have a communications department with a spokesperson who communicates on their behalf. This is for the purpose to release the latest updates about the company. Usually in the corporate world no one is authorized to speak on the company's behalf other than the spokesperson to insure that the right information is released.

If you are serious about winning you understand that it's apart of making something of yourself. Without the mean spirit of your haters, the good spirit of your purpose goes unnoticed. It's called bad press and good press. Bad press is when you're consistently put in situations that have a continual negative outcome. When your enemies can get close enough to expose your bad situations on an ongoing basis, that's when you have a big problem on your hands. Your haters should not know all of your natural shortcomings. Keep your haters on your radar so that you know what their doing at all times but keep them far enough so they cannot see all of your flaws.

A rumor is a current story or report circulating of uncertain or doubtful truth. The problem with chasing a story about you is that you don't know what portion of the story is truthful or has any truth to it at all. From the onset, you're not privy to that information and to get to the bottom of it will cost you too much time. Anything that has partial truth is still a lie and to chase a lie is below the winner. Winners are too busy accomplishing goals to run after something that has been fabricated.

There have been instances where I have personally addressed issues within my team with unauthorized people sharing information. This is a much different situation. Those who are close to you should understand the winners' policy. The winners' policy is that no information is communicated without official approval. The reason being is that some things are classified and classified information have the potential to be harmful to all parties due to sensitivity. That's the reason why the former NSA leaker Eric Snowden is wanted on espionage charges. It's also the reason why most companies who have a patent on their product require you to sign a document saying that you can never divulge what you really do for a living as it relates to their process.

## BRAND YOUR IDEA

I've stated many times that your business, company, or non-profit is your idea. Regardless of where you are with your idea, whether it's in preparation stage to be launched or already in existence, there is a proven formula to make it work. Here is what I called the "3D" strategy.

1. Build an identifiable logo that best fit your brand. In other word your logo should match the culture of your idea. Early on in my pastoring career, I didn't get this right, here's why. I built a culture of the church that was modern but when I designed the logo and had it created, it gave the perception that the church was your old school cathedral kind of church. It was a nice logo but it didn't fit the brand of our church. My particular flavor of ministry is more of the high energy, lights, camera action side of church and what the logo and my choice attire said was that there is some branding confusion.

When your idea's brand clashes with your its logo, you send a mix signal. Its then unclear to your audience as to what you or your idea is all about. This has to be carefully thought out. There has to be a consistent flow between your personal brand the company's brand and culture. Figure out what message you want to convey as it relates to your brand identity.

2. Your idea's brand should tell a story. Storytelling is a proven technique in branding an entity that tells a story through mass communication such as corporate logo, product, packaging and marketing materials. To the trained eye of the consumer, it will paint a picture of your Idea's product and expertise.

New York City realtor Michelle Allen, for example, only sell high-end condominiums in the upper eastside of Manhattan while most competitors sell real estate all over New York City. To illustrate and differentiate the aspect of her services or brand offer, a logo showing a New York City stationed next to central park is design for Allen's firm.

3. Brand naming is one of the most essential parts of branding your idea. Properly naming your brand will set the tone and personality of your idea, which will be the number one element in your mainstream marketing strategy. A name should be short and to the point and it should reflect the overall brand concept you've developed.

Choosing a name in a world of innovation and concepts can be rather difficult due to the wide variety that's currently used in existing registered trademarks. This problem is easy to fix by simply putting your desired name in a Google search will help you gauge whether or not to move forward with that name. Make sure that you check with respective trademark registries to insure your considered name isn't used and that the law protects you.

Here is a list of brand names in two different categories based on attributes that you can use as gauge when choosing your name.

Descriptive:

Names that say what the idea's brand do.

- Borders Books and Music
- Babies "R" Us
- Net Jets

Abstract:

Names that make no clear reference to the brand idea yet stands out.

- Yahoo
- Apple
- AOL

Choosing a designer or design firm will be important to your brand, as it will assist in establishing your idea's uniqueness that will cause it to stand out. A potential problem with start-up ideas could be their geographical location. If the start up is in a more smaller area, there a possibility that others brands use the same designer. The designer(s) are more of a local favorite among many. Most graphic designers have a particular flavor in which the untrained eye can detect. If everyone is using the same designer or design firm then your idea won't stand out from the rest. If is this is the case for you, reach outside and in list another designer even if it will cost you more.

A proven misunderstanding and one that designers are always forced to correct is that a brand is a logo or identity by itself, this is certainly not the case. Your logo is one outer expression of your brand. Your logo is graded as a top-level communication but not by itself. It's seen most frequently by the largest amount of people. All of your design elements should be a perfect mixture of your brand in a distinguishing marque.

In 1971 Bill Bowerman and Phil Knight founded a multinational sportswear company called Nike. They in listed Carolyn Davidson, a design student at Portland State University to design the logo. Davidson would eventually decide on the world famous Nike swoosh. From a designer's perspective, the swoosh is a simple abstract marque that communicates energy and movement which in this case is befitting for a brand that pioneers in sportswear.

# CODE NINE

# LAW & ORDER

*We hold these truths to be self-evident, that all men are created equal, that they are endowed by their creator with certain unalienable rights, that among these are life, liberty and the pursuit of happiness…*

*-Thomas Jefferson*

### ORDER

To understand the climate of which every structure such as family, business, educational institutions, government institutions, and houses of worship exists is to understand that no such entity can operate without order. For that matter, nothing can function properly without order.

The layers of the earth's crust have order. The layers of the human skin have order. The hemisphere is broken up into order. The alphabet has order. The number systems by which we get 1, 2, 3, 4, 5, are in systematic order.

Your responsibility to yourself, your family, and your legacy is to govern your life. Having order in your life will give you great advantages such as structure. Order will help you simplify things in your life by prioritizing, that means putting first things first. Order will help you manage home, work, and school properly.

Order is the sequence of things that are governed by principle or rule of law. The idea to have any success without some sort of order is an allusion. Everything has to have a higher principle as a point of reference to govern. The principle of a corporate structure is to have the CEO and management on all levels govern the company. The government of the company establishes and implement bylaws, rules and regulations where by the company can function. The same is with family; the original structural make up of family is to have a father and mother who govern the household including the children by establishing rules, chores, and direction.

As oxymoronic as it may sound, order enables certain groups like the mafia to "do wrong right". In other words, those who partake in organized crime understand that to do the wrong thing to produce a beneficial outcome requires order. Take a moment to study the five families, one in particular, the Gambino Family or the likes of Frank Lucas and the country boys, Nicky Barnes and the counsel. All of these organizations used order as a means of amassing great wealth and power. I do not endorse their crimes nor do agree with their reasoning, however, to ignore what order can do even in these situations would not be reasonable.

I saw a scene in the movie American Gangster, produced and starred by Denzel Washington. The death of notorious Bumpy Johnson who Lucas had worked for left the organization without a leader. Frank steps up to take control of the remains, to get a handle on the confusion, and to collect money owed to Johnson. This particular scene showed Washington as Frank Lucas meeting in a restaurant with a top-level mob boss exchanging what appeared to by a large amount of heroin. At this time, Lucas had not established the famous cadaver connection and was still purchasing his supply from the Italians.

As they sat at the table during the exchange, the Italian boss tell Lucas the difference in the way the African Americans ran organize crime and the way the Italians ran the business. The mob boss contended that the number one reason why the African American base organized crime had the high rate of division and confusion is because of the lack of order. "That will never happen with Italians" he said.

I thought after watching that scene, what a powerful message. Order has power to enable that, which was never meant to have mobility. Order can put structure to something that is considered to be illegal and make it work as if it was a fortune five hundred company. It causes me to wonder how much more can order do if we as a people can adopt and actually put it to work in our lives.

The direct opposite of order is chaos. Chaos is a word to describe craziness and confusion. Synonyms for the word chaos are disarray, mayhem, bedlam, pandemonium, havoc, turmoil, commotion, disruption, upheaval, uproar, mess, and free for all. When order is removed from something, chaos will soon follow. Whenever you can associate these words to any part of your life, there is the absence of order. To exist in such space is unproductive and unhealthy, for the absence of order will lead one on a downward spiral to insanity.

In an ever-changing world where order is no longer a commodity, I submit to you that if you want to win, you must go through every aspect of your life and where there is chaos, simply put order to it. Here are some ways you can.

I am amazed as I go into the personal space of others of how cluttered their lives are. Setting order can be something as simple removing clutter from your personal space such as your house, car or even your office. You can start with your closet with three simple steps. First, pick up everything and whatever you no longer wear, donate it to your local goodwill or Salvation Army. Second, pair all shirts with shirts, pants with pants, suits with suits, dresses with dresses and so on. Third, color coordinate everything. For extra storage purchase tub-a-wear.

Another example of how you can set order to your life is creating a routine. A routine is a sequence of actions you regularly follow. A generic routine for anyone could consist of waking up early in the morning, working out, eating a healthy breakfast, taking a shower and off to work. Your daily routine should be one that is tailored made to your lifestyle and is one that your do religiously. This helps you maintain a level of commitment to your overall goals. Using the generic routine I gave you, by waking up early and working out will help you reach your ultimate goal to loose weight or stay in shape.

Cutting back on the use of electronics will assist in creating order to our life. I know that in a world of technology that this can be rather difficult and one of my personal challenges. Technology is one of society's greatest friends yet it can easily turn into an enemy. The excessive use of electronics has a way of detaching us from the real world.

Most can agree that they have more two or more forms of electronics. One day while sitting in the coffee shop, I took notice to the fact that I had a MacBook, iPad, and iPhone there present with me. The reality of all three devices I had in my possession is they are essentially the same device in different form and had the same functions. Because I am a "techy" at heart, I almost neglected to see how engrossed my life is with technology gadgets. This is an easy distraction when it isn't properly used.

Social media sites such as Twitter, Facebook, Instagram, Tumblr, Pinterest, and LinkedIn can also be easy distractions if not properly managed. Do a survey on how much time our of a twenty-four hour day do you frequent these sites. If most of your down time consist of the use of these sites, you certainly want to correct this by setting an amount of time during the day that you use these sites.

Negativity is a contagious disease that is passed on from one person to another. One of many challenges you will face while applying the winners' code is negativity. Removing negativity from your life will be sure to help you establish order. Sometimes this means removing negative people from you're life and as far as family and friends, its ok to put a hold on your associations with them until they are ready to honor where your going.

If you ever take a moment to study what make most people successful you will see undoubtedly that all of them have mastered this thing called order. All of them have some sort of routine that keeps them prepared and on schedule. I know that you intend to champion life in every area or else you would have not read this book this far, I contend that order is by far one of the top priorities for the winner.

To have the audacity to challenge every dysfunctional aspect of your life by placing order will cost you. I must to tell you this so that you know up front and you are not caught by surprise when things dramatically change. You see it's the same as eating at a five-star restaurant. The cost of eating the best is expensive but what you ORDER, you pay for.

## GOVERNMENT

The word government in Greek form means rights of citizen; Hebrew, rule and dominion. In the United States, it is principle authority made up of multiple branches, that being the United States Senate and United States House of Representatives. The President of the United States leads the two branches. It is the function of the U.S. Supreme Court to hold both branches and the President accountable. In other countries such as England, parliament would be their official form of government.

The Honorable Ezra Taft Benson former Secretary of Agriculture under the Eisenhower administration held that "governments was instituted of God for the benefit of mankind; and that he holds men accountable for the acts in relations to them, both in making laws and administering them, for the good and safety for all society. No government can exist in peace, except such laws are framed and held inviolate as will to secure to each individual the free exercise of conscience, the right and control of property, and protection of life".

Understanding how government works will help you in many ways. Mainly, it will keep you abreast on your legal right to win in areas such as taxes and loopholes, local and federal laws that affect you, constitutional laws like the first amendment which protects our right to the freedom of religion, freedom of speech and freedom of press. Once government is understood then you can apply the model to your personal life and the rest is history.

What keeps the rich, rich and the poor, poor is the proper understanding of government and its roll. Government have many benefits that everyday citizens are not aware of or do not take advantage of. Such benefits as tax loopholes, various business corporation filings such as an LLP or LLC, grants, loans, disaster relief funds, mortgage assistant programs, renters assistance, etc. Most people view bankruptcy as some shameful experience rather than a federal debt relief law. You would be shocked of how many influential businessmen and woman take advantage of such laws to help them and there companies stay on the winning team.

President John F. Kennedy said in his 1961 inaugural address " ask not what your country can do for you, ask what you can do for your country". While I am a firm believer of his philosophy, I am also interested in a mutual exchange. It is the function of government to protect the welfare of all of its citizens.

I believe we can all agree that the purpose of government is to secure the rights and freedoms of every individual citizen. Rights are legal, social, or ethical principles of freedom and entitlement. These rights are found in laws that were previously created and those that are in current development. If we neglect to protect, uphold, and obey the law, then we stand to put it in the hands of those who do not wish to keep it in the favor for all but rather turn it in the favor of the nations' elite.

## DYSFNCTIONAL GOVERNMENT

The primary problem we have in the world today is the dissatisfaction with government. It is displayed in a variety of forms and most notably the rise in protest against government. People all over the world are demanding purity from their respective governments. The international community is opposing rogued political leaders, the lack of transparency, honesty, social injustice, trust, and faith.

We saw it in America with the protest of Obamacare. We saw it in Libya with the reign of terror of President Muammar Gaddafi, which eventually led to his capture and death. We saw it in Egypt on two separate occasions. We saw it in Syria with the country in objection to President Bashar al-Assad and most recently the protest of the former Ukrainian Government that forced out President Viktor Yanukovych.

The dissatisfaction of government has often left these countries in a civil war. At the helm of democracy, we've seen governments use military force against the very citizens it was designed to protect. The use of chemical weapons has even been used in one case such as the crisis in Syria. Governments that have been tainted will do anything to threaten democracy and the welfare of its citizens, particularly those who demand accountability.

My conclusion of global assessment is that the modern day governments that were established to be problem solvers have become the problem. The results have been staggering as people cry out all over the globe with a relentless spirit to fight even under the notion that their lives could be lost. Exercising the right to vote and winning elections is one thing and actually having a healthy government is another.

## GOVERNMENT & RACISM

The role of government was designed to promise domestic tranquility by insuring all who were created equally have an equal shot at the American dream. Regrettably when our constitution was enacted, it seemed to be a mere prophesy of the things to come Instead of the existing reality. The truth is that when our constitution was created in 1787 and ratified in 1788, our country was still very much one that did not recognize all people as being equal. We were deeply engrossed in slavery and in an ironic twist; our very own forefathers were slaves owners themselves. So then it makes me wonder, whom did the constitution really recognize as people if Africans or African Americans were not considered as being created equally according to the very ones who wrote it? Were African Americans considered to be anything other than of the human race?

It is from this early mindset that racism and inequality were embedded through generations of people that span thousands of years. Like it or not, America is still a very racist country even with an African American President and century and a half since slavery ended. Amazingly, people who are suppose to be equal with all of humanity still have the twisted ideologies passed down from those who preceded them hundreds of years before their existence. For heavens' sake, these individuals inherited and employ such ignorance from those whom they have never even met.

Like many who were upset with President Lincoln during the time when he wanted to abolish slavery, so is the same resistance to do away with racism and discrimination today. Those who fought for freedom on the frontline are still fighting from the grave. We have come a long way but the race isn't finished. It would be a tragedy to come up with a modern day proclamation emancipation just to abolish what has long been the greatest genocide against mankind.

While putting the finishing touches on this book in preparations to send it to print, I received a news update on my iPhone about the owner of the Los Angeles Clippers of the NBA. I was stunned at what I was watching after reports surfaced of owner Donald Sterling ranting about his then girlfriend not posting pictures on her social media page with blacks. Here is a guy who has a number of Blacks and Hispanics that play on his team, yet he still possess a modern day plantation style mindset. That's not all; just in 2009 he settled a lawsuit against him that claimed he had tried to push out all minorities out of his Los Angeles properties, and to think that this is 2014 with such ignorant behavior is appalling.

More stories are coming out about how the sick mentality of modern day slavery are seeping out of people who refuse to see all mankind as one. Although we have an African American President, Attorney General, a host of influential African American and Hispanic icons, millionaires, and billionaires, we must ask ourselves how far have we come? With such racism and discriminatory thinking, exactly how far are we from the

Jackie Robison story or perhaps from the civil rights movement? How much closer are we to the American dream?

In a land where such toxic thinking have been for centuries dividing the states by diving the people, should we rely on the progress of government or the fundamentals upon which it was created to once and for all eradicate such ideology? I submit that until we can find away to do so, we will never reach the American dream.

Between the Constitution and those who wrote and agreed to it, there was a great deal hypocrisy. It's like writing a journal entry about your day with the facts of the day being distorted or a made up fictional story of how your day is suppose to be. Reality and prophecy are vastly different.

Moreover, while government didn't, in my view, believe all of what it had established at the time, I believe that it was still inspired by God and that He is all knowing. I believe that the constitution was perfectly stated even in a racially imperfect time. In full circle the law had to favor all race, religion, creed, social, and financial backgrounds. Again, it is government's role to ensure that there is liberty and justice for all who are created equal.

## GOVERNMENT & RELIGION

I personally support government not infringing upon religious organizations as historically interpreted by constitutional law. However, I am not in support of the separation of church and state as modern culture seeks to interpret it as to remove God from every form of government. The fundamentals of our very constitution were built on the faith and convictions our forefathers. Despite our country's motto referencing our trust as a nation to God or God existing in our pledge of allegiance and God being printed on our currency, progressive anti- religious groups still petition the high courts to abolish such principles. Therefore, the separation between "church and state" is often confused with "God and state".

All faiths speak of the order of government. I believe the reason is that regardless of ideas of who God is, God himself when creating the universe established it for a reason. The scriptures tell the Christian in Romans 13 to obey the laws of the land. The Qur'an in verse 4:59 tells the Muslim to obey those that have rulership. The Vedas tell the Hindu in Yama 8 to obey the laws of the nation or locale, to name a few.

One of my biggest challenges with those of my faith is the lack of attention or relevance to government as if governmental affairs do not affect Christians. When the prophet Isaiah foretold of Jesus thousands of years in advanced, He recorded that His name would be called wonderful, counselor, mighty God, everlasting father and that the government shall be on his shoulder. Take notice to the words counselor and government. A counselor is one who argues the point of law. I'm inclined to believe that government as prescribed in Isaiah's foreshadow means that the mindset of Christ is governmental order. That order than brings about peace and prosperity.

All through out the Bible are references to law and order like the twenty-four elders. These elders are referred to as ruling elders. The New Testament of scripture refers to prayer as a petition. Jesus' first sermon was for us to repent meaning change the way we think and turn completely around for the kingdom of God is at hand. The word "kingdom" is a form of government. Jesus also states that he did not come to do away with the law. The Ten Commandments are nothing more than a set of laws.

My question is how than can we as a people have little to no regard to the divine structure and order of government? Why do we hide behind cultural negligence as a means to why we disavow our innate rights? Are we so busy with religious affairs that we cannot see that both religion and government go hand and hand?

The totality of all that I've mentioned up to this point is a combination of why the world system is off balance. For there to be peace and prosperity for all, there must be a joint effort between the market place, religion and government.

Thaddeus Parker is a highly sought after motivational speaker, enlightened lecturer, and rising voice for the next generation. His love for people has given him inspiration to cross religious, market place and political lines to transform lives with the message of winning.

Parker is the CEO of TDP Holdings LLC. a world class company with diverse interest in strategic investments.

As a licensed minister and former senior pastor, he enjoys sharing his faith with people from all walks of life through public speaking and annual champion gatherings.

For booking and more information on upcoming tour dates log on to thaddeusparker.com and connect with him on:
twitter.com/thaddeusparker
facebook.com/thaddeusparker
instagram.com/thaddeusdparker

## THE PRAYER OF SALVATION

Father in Jesus name, I acknowledge that I am a sinner. I believe that your only begotten son Jesus Christ died on a cross at Calvary for my sins. Today I turn from my sins and receive your forgiveness. Thank you for saving me.

Amen.

# THADDEUS PARKER

## BOOK RESEARCH SOURCE GUIDE

All scripture quoted in this book is from the King James Version unless otherwise noted.

Most research for this book was done via internet. Notable sites our as follows:

Secretary Ezra T. Benson
http://www.laissez-fairerepublic.com/benson.htm

President Franklin D. Roosevelt
http://historymatters.gmu.edu/d/5057/
http://whitehouse.gov

The Great Depression
http://www.history.com/topics/great-depression

Wikipedia.com

All rights reserved.

www.ingramcontent.com/pod-product-compliance
Lightning Source LLC
LaVergne TN
LVHW051832080426
835512LV00018B/2831